ME,
MYSELF
&IDEAS

ME, MYSELF & IDEAS

THE ULTIMATE GUIDE TO BRAINSTORMING SOLO

CARRIE ANTON AND JESSICA NORDSKOG

Andrews McMeel
PUBLISHING®

CONTENTS

Introduction

BRAINSTORMING SOLO?

THE IDEA OF "brainstorming solo" may seem, on its surface, like nonsense. When we think of innovation, we tend to imagine teams of people collaborating to solve creative conundrums. While we've got nothing against collaboration, we know that in today's working world, it's common to find yourself operating solo—commuting by phone or video-chat or working from home as a freelancer or small-business solopreneur. If this is you, then you know how important—and how difficult!—it is to keep the creativity flowing and the ideas fresh.

Whether you're an artist, freelance writer, consultant, or small-business owner, you're probably also familiar with regular spells of self-doubt and creative stalling. What may seem like a manageable problem to the traditional worker can easily trigger a crisis for someone whose office is also her living room. That's where this book comes in.

As solopreneurs ourselves, we're big believers in the power of one. Whether you've been working solo for years now or only recently parted with your nine-to-five, you've likely been thinking and creating independently for longer than you realize. Your ideas brought you this far, and we're gonna take a wild guess this isn't where your path ends. Perhaps you're stuck on a particular problem or you're having trouble deciding which idea of yours is worth the effort. Maybe you're experiencing a creative dry spell or feeling overwhelmed by distractions.

By the end of this book, you'll be armed with a set of diverse techniques for firing up creativity, generating and selecting your best ideas, and navigating all manner of obstacles—all by yourself. You'll also (we hope) feel a little less alone on your solo journey.

BEYOND THE PLUNGE

If you're like most solopreneurs, you've probably read plenty of books about taking control of your destiny, coming up with small-biz ideas, understanding the legalities involved, and mustering the motivation and self-confidence to chase those dreams. And then it's all: "Yes! You did it! You are now your own boss!"

This isn't that kind of book.

We're more concerned with what comes *after* that initial plunge. Perhaps the only thing tougher than striking out on your own is persevering when business starts to wane or your ideas feel stale or a changing market has you scrambling to adapt.

Worry not, friend. You've come to the right place.

Here's what to expect in the pages to follow.

WAIT, BUT . . . AM I MISSING OUT?

Yes, in fact, you are. Let's take a moment to acknowledge what you'll lose—and gain—by skipping the group brainstorm.

THE "BIG TALKER"

Every brainstorm has one—the guy (or gal!) who thinks they have all the ideas. So many ideas, in fact, they just can't stop talking, and no one else has a chance to contribute.

COOTIES!

Two words: flu season. The flu shot is great, but avoiding people altogether is way more effective. Much like children, shared whiteboard markers are like little germ factories.

STICKY FINGERS

There will always be that coworker who tries to claim your best ideas as his or her own. When it's just you in the brainstorming session, your ideas are safe from being stolen.

BUSINESS CASUAL

Lose the pantsuit—heck, lose the pants altogether! As a solo brainstormer, you're free to think, create, and conduct business in your comfiest outfit, which just might be your birthday suit.

YOUR BRAINSTORMING AGENDA

SECTION ONE: *Greetings & Ground Rules*

Just as traditional group brainstorms tend to start off with a preview of what's to come and a meet and greet with company peers, this introductory section welcomes you to your own solo brainstorm. And instead of going around the room to say your name, your department, and your favorite cafeteria meal, you're about to get to know yourself a whole lot better.

But we can't move on without some rules first! Maybe the most common ground rule of every good brainstorm is "There are no bad ideas." And barring clear plastic mom-jeans, we couldn't agree more. But when you're solostorming, the ground rules change a bit. This section is dedicated to laying down your own laws and enforcing them like a boss.

SECTION TWO: *The Breakout*

The go-to mantra for real estate agents is "Location. Location. Location." And it applies just as well to brainstorming. When it comes to generating ideas, where you do it makes all the difference to what you develop. Just as your office space shouldn't make work painful, your brainstorming space shouldn't discourage creativity. That doesn't mean hiring an interior designer, but it may mean getting out to take in a change of scenery or discovering the creative potential of the chaos that is your office.

SECTION THREE: *Icebreakers*

Gone are the games designed to make group attendees feel more comfortable but that do just the opposite. You know what we're talking about: Two Truths and a Lie, a BINGO card filled with interests and character traits to match to other meeting-goers, or a charades-style game with animal noises and movements the rest of the group has to guess—because nothing says "not awkward" like mooing and mock chewing cud in front of your peers. Good news: not one of those awful games will be recommended here! Instead, this section is nothing but fun warm-ups you can use to transition from get-work-done mode to the brainstorm-brilliant-ideas zone. The goal of the exercises featured is to get your brain working in new ways while helping to prep yourself for your upcoming brainstorm sessions. It's sort of a two-for-one: power down the business brain and gear up for killer creativity.

SECTION FOUR: Brainstorm

Let the ideating begin! Unlike the icebreaker exercises and activities, which were designed to shake free everyday burdens, this section homes in on generating ideas and solving your solopreneur problems. The 20 techniques provided will guide you through any creative conundrum, process problem, or general feeling of stuckness, with methods you can modify to suit your needs.

SECTION FIVE: Sit & Simmer

Ideas need time to incubate before going primetime. That's because what you thought was a brilliant idea at first might actually be a logistical nightmare, or not profitable, or just plain dumb. The thing is you don't know how good an idea is until you've sat on it a while. And unless you were gifted with the rare virtue of patience (full disclosure: we weren't), waiting is tough. This section not only makes the downtime easier but also gives your brain a mental break after all that intense creative work. Here, we offer exercises and activities to help you endure the waiting period while also prepping your brain for what's up next.

SECTION SIX: Debrief

Brainstorming groups often welcome this end-of-meeting chat, as it means they can soon go back to surfing the web at their desks instead of using up mobile data to scroll through social media. But for you, the work has only just begun. You now have ideas . . . and ones that don't make you cringe even after some downtime and a meal. So, what now?

This section helps you better assess, form, and broaden your ideas so that you can decide which ones will go on to star in your work life. And since there are bound to be bumps in the road with any idea you have, this section will also offer valuable problem-solving tips and resources so that you don't feel stranded.

Lastly, we'll give an overview of how to keep the creative candle burning bright, with suggestions for developing a daily creative habit for nonstop ideas whenever you need them.

Meet Your Facilitators

WE'RE THE WONDER WOMEN! That is, the two-woman team—Carrie and Jessica—who founded the brainstorming business Wonder: An Idea Studio.

Wonder was born as we both looked to escape the nine-to-five and make a go at solo gigs. We knew we were destined to do something creative, a passion we'd both been honing since before our time as editors at Mattel's American Girl. There, Carrie wrote, edited, and styled for the doll company's contemporary line of advice and activity books, while Jessica did the same for *American Girl* magazine before moving on to design the brand's iconic toy products.

As we set out to start our own business, we realized we had more ideas than we knew what to do with. And that's when our "aha" moment happened: *we were idea people!* Since before we can remember, we've been thinking about the next big thing. And so, Wonder: An Idea Studio came to be.

When we went solo with Wonder, we had to expand our skill sets and develop strategies for addressing topics, challenges, and industries that were wholly new to us.

Sure, we were nervous that our brains wouldn't be up to the task. But instead of dwelling on feeling out of our element, we discovered that the brainstorming techniques we'd already honed could easily be adapted for our changing needs. In short, we had unlocked our superpower!

Ideas are what we do; they're what we know. And we've made a career out of helping others unlock their own ideas. As Wonder Women, our goal is to show you that the idea-generating superpower lies within you, too. Let's tap into it and bring your ideas to life!

1

GREETINGS & GROUND RULES

IT'S TIME TO MEET YOUR IDEA MAKER . . .
YOU! LET'S GET THIS PARTY OF ONE STARTED.

QUIZ:

HELLO
MY NAME IS

NOW THAT YOU know us, it's time for you to get to know yourself. After all these years of being you, you may think you know yourself better than anyone else. And true as that may be, how well do you really know your inner brainstormer?

If you two are truly besties, feel free to skip ahead to the Ground Rules. Otherwise, it's time to procrastinate with a quiz.

#1. MY TO-DO LIST GENERALLY LOOKS LIKE A . . .

A. high-level view of the goals I want to achieve in my business that week.

B. bulleted list organized by the top tasks to check off that day. Any items not completed will be promptly placed as top priority on the next day's list.

C. list of people with whom to connect, social media content to post and share, and daily blogs to read so that I can stay current on what's happening.

D. replica of the daily activities iconic business owners and CEOs do, according to the articles I've read. To be the best, you have to think like the best. I'm on my way!

E. bunch of random sticky notes posted around my office and house, or wherever the thoughts come to mind.

#2. THE WEEKEND IS ALMOST HERE! WHAT DOES YOURS LOOK LIKE?

A. A perfectly executed weekend of fun out of town. My goal this year is to collect memories, not things. Check!

B. Like every other weekend: hot yoga on Saturday morning followed by grocery shopping and walking the dog. I'll have dinner out then sleep in on Sunday morning. If it's not in my routine, I'm not interested.

C. Full! I've already texted friends to meet for dinner on Friday. Saturday is spa day with my sister. Sunday starts with brunch and ends with a football party starring the neighborhood gang at my house.

D. After a serious sweat session in spin class, I'm headed to my college friend's place for a networking brunch. Later, I'm also hoping to finish reading a really inspiring biography and stream a webinar or two.

E. I like to take it as it comes. I have a few tentative plans, but I might bail and instead take a nice long walk and a nap.

#3. MY IDEA OF CLOTHING SHOPPING IS . . .

A. any kind of subscription service where I can show them my style and they send it directly to my door.

B. researching different stores online to find exactly what I want at the right value. I prefer to have it shipped directly to me, but I'll make the trek out if trying something on or making sure a color matches will save me time and money.

C. a day in the city visiting the newest shops with my friends. The more opinions of purchases I get (and can give!) the better.

D. trying out new, locally owned stores. Not only does it help me to build a standout style but also I can connect with other small-business owners.

E. nonexistent. I have plenty of clothes, but I guess if I need something, a secondhand store is more my vibe.

#4. MY PASSPORT IS . . .

A. stamped with all of the continental European countries from when I studied abroad in college. I had to cram it all in so I could focus on my career upon graduating.

B. stamped with only a few, very carefully chosen countries. It takes a lot of planning to execute a well-rounded vacation overseas.

C. stamped with only English-speaking countries. If I can't talk to the locals, what's the point?

D. ready and waiting. I've registered for two business conferences so that I can use my work to check off my travel bucket list.

E. around here somewhere. If the opportunity to travel drops in my lap, I'll find it. Otherwise, there are plenty of off the beaten paths to explore close to home.

#5. THE FIRST THING I DO WHEN I WAKE UP IS . . .

A. exercise my body and mind by combining fitness with visualization techniques.

B. strategically plan out my to-do list and then set to work checking off tasks.

C. scroll through my social media accounts, commenting, liking, and sharing as I go.

D. repeat my daily mantra, "Dream it. Do it."

E. press snooze a couple of times and slowly stretch as I think about my first cup of coffee.

#6. MY FAVORITE KIND OF MOVIE IS . . .

A. a legal thriller. I love to see powerful, smart people in action.

B. a complex murder mystery where the facts are presented like a puzzle for me to solve.

C. filled with the biggest celebs in Hollywood. Following them on social media isn't enough; seeing them on the big screen makes me feel like we're hanging out together.

D. a documentary about a rags-to-riches success story. I love an underdog who overcomes all odds.

E. a comedy. Who wants to do anything else but laugh till it hurts during a movie?

#7. WHICH ONE BEST DESCRIBES YOUR LEADERSHIP STYLE?

A. Put me front and center. I'm a true leader of the pack.

B. Tell me what's the endgame, and I'll devise a plan to delegate tasks to get the job done.

C. I prefer to take a twist on "lead by example." By that I mean I look to other people for examples, then I take the lead.

D. I'm still a member of the pack, but I'm doing my best to prove there's room for me at the top.

E. Is "go with the flow" a leadership style?

#8. WHEN CHOOSING A RESTAURANT, I . . .

A. pick a place not just for the food but for the overall dining experience.

B. go with what I know. If a place serves a dish I consistently like, I eliminate the risk of a food fail.

C. am all about the scene and the prettiest plate of food possible. After all, I can get more likes when I make my social followers drool.

D. look for shared tables so that I can strike up conversations with new people. You never know the influential and important people you might meet while you eat.

E. prefer places with tasty eats nearest to where I am when hunger strikes.

#9. MY IDEAL METHOD OF TRANSPORTATION IS . . .

A. a versatile car that fits my changing needs, no matter what they may be.

B. a carpool. I not only can save on gas and mileage but also enjoy organizing the schedule.

C. a model with a little razzle dazzle. I love to catch the eye of passersby, plus it makes the perfect spot for selfies.

D. public transportation. While a luxury car would be nice, learning about others' career paths while getting around beats sitting alone.

E. my bike or hitching a ride with a buddy. Traffic is just too much of a headache to handle.

#10. WHEN IT COMES TO KEEPING ORGANIZED FOR WORK, I CAN'T LIVE WITHOUT . . .

A. my virtual assistant. I can get more done when I invest in good help from others.

B. my daily planner. It holds my entire life, and I'd be lost without it.

C. my phone. It gives me the whole world at my fingertips.

D. apps. There are so many great apps that smart people have created to make life easier.

E. sticky notes. They're perfect for appointment reminders, grocery lists, and remembering to throw away the leftovers before they stink up my fridge.

#11. WHEN PLANNING A PARTY, I . . .

A. hire an event planner. I want someone with whom I can share my vision and make it come to life.

B. merge an all-encompassing to-do list with a calendar of deadlines to pull off every detail of the party spotlessly.

C. book a party room at a restaurant where the work is done for me so that I can spend time socializing with the guests and having a blast.

D. stick to events that are less about the party and more about the connections. I did enough keg stands in college; it's time to get to work.

E. let it happen organically. If a group of people ends up at my house, we'll order some takeout food and make a wine run.

ANSWERS:

CHARLIE IN CHARGE

If you answered **mostly As**, then you're the boss. Not just the boss of your business and the work you do but also the boss of big ideas. Liken your inner brainstormer to a CEO armed with years of knowledge and experience and a natural leader's intuition. You both observe the world around you and rise to the challenge of making it a better place.

While some may view these traits as intimidating, the confidence you possess is a reminder of your greatness. But as Uncle Ben said to Peter Parker (a.k.a. Spider-Man): "With great power there must also come great responsibility." You understand this responsibility, and thus, the risks you take are calculated ones. Your brainstorming is characterized by realistic optimism—you're always balancing big dreams with the big picture.

As you move forward with the exercises in this book, challenge yourself to leave reality behind and float toward pie-in-the-sky ideas like an untethered balloon in the Macy's Thanksgiving Day Parade. Rise like Snoopy. Float like Big Bird. And touch the wild blue yonder like the inflated Hello Kitty you know you are.

PRACTICAL PEYTON

If you answered **mostly Bs**, you're a (wo)man with a plan and you're ready to lead the way. A master middle manager, you're the one others turn to when it's time to get work done. When a project falls on your plate, you jump in like an Iron Chef, wielding freshly sharpened knives to slice and dice the big-picture goal into a step-by-step strategy anyone could follow. You keep your proverbial kitchen running like a well-oiled machine, making sure to motivate as needed and remove any obstacles standing in your way.

Despite your solopreneur mind-set, you approach your work as though your various hats represent members of a team coming together to complete a task. As the supervisor of this formidable "group," you have the fortitude to lead the way. Remember, though, when it comes to ideas, it's OK to deviate from the path paved and wander down roads less traveled.

As you move forward with the exercises in this book, envision yourself the contestant in a game show. Skip playing it safe and going home with the $250, and instead go for what's behind door 2. Maybe a stinker awaits. However, if you never try, you're guaranteed to never feel the spray of the cool ocean waves on the back of your . . . brand . . . new . . . JET SKI!

SOCIAL SYDNEY

If you answered **mostly Cs**, you're great at getting the gab going, as you always have something to say. The super-social coworker, you're the person others go to when they want to know what's going on—the person with the pulse on what's trending, who's hot and who's not, and what's happening close to home. You're always happy to dish on which celeb couple is headed toward splitsville, who in your social circle has a bun in the oven, and what new app is going to revolutionize how people keep in touch.

Some may consider you the town gossip, but you prefer to think of yourself as an exceptionally curious creature, eager to see and experience as much as you can. Despite your tendency to feel inspired by everything around you, generating new ideas doesn't always come easily. Comparison mode kicks in quickly, and you start to worry your ideas can't compete with what someone else posts in their social feed. Because you're so focused on the outside world, sometimes you forget to look within and trust your gut.

As you move forward with the exercises in this book, find moments for quiet in your life. We don't mean you should spend every waking hour at the library. Instead, take a few minutes (or longer!) each day to power down and take a break from your busyness and a world that can't stop talking. Sit in the sunshine (with sunscreen on, of course), take a tree-hugging hike through the woods, or just be still, doing nothing at all. It will feel foreign at first, but the more silence you create, the more space there is for new ideas to sneak a word in edgewise.

ROOKIE RORY

If you answered **mostly Ds**, you're like a baby deer taking wobbly steps for the first time. One day—possibly as soon as tomorrow—you'll be the majestic creature you've dreamed of. For now, Bambi, you're experiencing the forest for what may feel like the first time. In the traditional corporate world, consider yourself on par with the intern or new employee. You have something to prove, and you yearn to learn and absorb as much as you can in order to make the biggest impact possible.

While you are filled with a bevy of ideas, try to reign in your eagerness. Your hard work and dedication will surely be an asset in whatever you set out to do, but that doesn't mean you need to force ideas just for the sake of having them. That said, you don't have to dam the stream of consciousness either.

HELLO
MY NAME IS
ROOKie RORY

As you move forward with the exercises in this book, seek the survival skills necessary to find your way in the wild. The forest contains many paths, some of which offer easy terrain, while others follow steep inclines. When the going gets rough, rely on your forest friends to show you the way. Once you've learned from the masters, begin to explore on your own.

LAID-BACK LOGAN

If you answered **mostly Es**, you're probably wondering why brainstorming is even a thing. After all, your best ideas seem to fall from the sky like pennies from heaven. Take a shower, get an idea. Dream at night, get another idea. Ride the subway, boom—more ideas! Forcing ideas to come your way seems like a lot more work than you have the energy to undertake.

Your carefree ways are coveted by your more stress-prone comrades, but don't let yourself get lazy. It's super cool that you receive ideas like most of us receive junk mail. But it's easy to take ideas—and hordes of mailers—for granted. If you let them pile up, they'll eventually be trashed.

As you move forward with the exercises in this book, think of idea generation like running a hotel. Keep rooms available for wanted (and, at times, unwanted) guests. Be the host(ess) with the most(est), entertaining any visitor who walks through the door looking for a place to crash. Offer a turndown service in your smartest suite, give full access to the minibar, and treat your idea-

HELLO
MY NAME IS
LAID-BACK LOGAN

guests with the respect everyone deserves. If you develop a connection, comp their next night—or ask them to room with you forever. Create some good idea karma by never turning your back on a visitor because you believe (foolishly) they'll drop in again next week. Instead, leave your patrons—your ideas—with a sweet parting message: "Y'all come back now, ya hear?"

GROUND RULES

WHEN YOU'RE BRAINSTORMING on your own instead of in a group, the rules of the game need to change. Since no one will be there to call you out, ring a bell, or send you back to your stuffy cubicle for breaking the rules, we're employing the honor system to keep things civilized.

RULE #1: *Unplug.* Nothing can bust a brainstorm—not to mention a small business—faster than negative comparisons. You may think good ideas are best influenced by other ideas, but when you're on hour three of scrolling Instagram, feeling too overwhelmed by others' apparent success to move, you'll know how wrong you were. So unless you're just out to drool over your foodie friends' fancy meal pictures, stay off social media until the idea generating is done.

RULE #2: *No judging.* You know how you feel about yourself on the not-so-fun morning after an oh-so-fun night with friends and cocktails? Yeah—no bueno. When it comes to brainstorming, don't apply that level of judgment to the ideas you develop. Basically, no self-shaming allowed.

RULE #3: *Remember, there are no bad ideas.* OK, technically, there are bad ideas. Otherwise, every idea that occurred to someone would become a thing. But if you dismiss every idea as "bad" before giving it a chance to prove itself, you'll have no ideas from which to choose. Furthermore, just because you think it's a bad idea now doesn't mean others won't love it. For instance, in 2016, people voted online to name a $287-million government-funded polar research ship the "R.S.S. Boaty McBoatface."[1] What may seem foolish today could be tomorrow's viral sensation.

RULE #4: *Let it grow.* Ideas are a lot like infants. In the beginning, they're small, cute, and interesting—but also kind of dumb and useless and needy. Like babies, ideas make you question everything you do, rob you of sleep, and lead you to look differently at the surrounding world. For the same reasons parents reproduce, you generate ideas: to create a legacy, change the world, and maybe have a funding source to pay for the nursing home one day. Most babies can't achieve those goals while still drooling and wearing diapers, but nurture them and let them grow, and they can do all that and more. So can ideas.

RULE #5: *Be a goal digger.* Brainstorming without parameters can feel like floating out to sea without a lifeline. Pick a time limit, idea quantity, or other goal to reach for so that the tide of creativity doesn't swallow you whole.

RULE #6: *Take a nap.* Because, damn it, that's one of the solopreneur perks you exchanged for a steady paycheck! And really, when all else fails and you can't come up with one single idea, naps can help press the reset button on your brain. Seriously. Researchers at the University of California, Riverside, have determined that a 90-minute nap can lead to similar learning benefits—a must for creativity—as those produced by a full night's sleep.[2] Don't have that long? Another study shows that even a 10-minute power nap can help you feel restored and boost your performance.

RULE #7: *Take a shower.* Studies show that getting naked leads to better ideas. OK, we made that up, but the surprising number of good ideas that arrive in the shower makes it a strong hypothesis. So if you wake up from your nap feeling not-so-refreshed, take it all off and head to the shower. If nothing else, your roommate or spouse will appreciate a less funky you. A win-win.

RULE #8: *Be kind, but don't rewind.* Let's face it: some days are diamonds, and some days are rocks. If you're having a "rock" kind of day and you're just not feelin' it, then take a break. Be kind to your creative soul (who is normally a total workhorse). Accept that you're not going to have a marathon of genius ideas and move on. Did you hear us? Move on! Don't dwell on it and do something else. Tomorrow (or later today, after that 10- or 90-minute nap) is a new day in the realm of ideas.

RULE #9: *Treat yo' self.* First, see Rule #1. Now go shopping for the best pen and notebook you can find. You know that haute leather notebook that's been calling to you from the overpriced boutique window? Buy it now. That beautiful paper and pen will be begging you to use them.

RULE #10: *Take it with you.* The best part about being a solo brainstormer is that you can generate ideas wherever you are. You probably always have your smartphone handy, but don't forget to bring your fancy notebook and pen wherever you go, too. Ideas are all around you—even in the waiting room at the doctor's office. Getting out of your normal setting can often spur an idea, so don't miss an opportunity to jot one down or snap a pic.

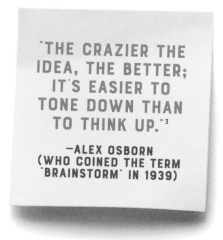

"THE CRAZIER THE IDEA, THE BETTER; IT'S EASIER TO TONE DOWN THAN TO THINK UP."[3]

—ALEX OSBORN (WHO COINED THE TERM "BRAINSTORM" IN 1939)

2 THE BREAKOUT

DESIGN YOUR VERY OWN

IDEA DEN.

SET THE SCENE

IDEAS ARE A lot like shooting stars; they're exciting when they happen, but you can't count on them showing up when and where needed.

Without a shooting star, your next-best option is to entice ideas out of hiding—which requires setting the scene. In group brainstorm sessions, it's not uncommon for teams to choose unconventional venues. Instead of stiff boardrooms or conference-style setups, the brainstorm might take place in a cozy lobby with comfy couches, bright natural light, plenty of snacks, and tactile toys to keep restless bodies busy.

And when businesses really get behind the importance of big ideas, they'll often send teams off-site to brainstorm in locations new and unique. With an estimated 3.7 million American employees telecommuting as of 2017, you might assume the appeal of leaving campus is no longer really relevant.[1] In reality, changing your environment—whether you're getting out of the office or getting out of the house—can ultimately help to change the way you think. A new space can equal new ideas—and lots of them.

BRAINSTORM ANYWHERE . . . BUT NOT EVERYWHERE

Thanks to laptops, tablets, smartphones, and Bluetooth, it's possible to work just about anywhere: airports, coffee shops, bedrooms, couches, beaches, and the list goes on. If you've got Wi-Fi, you can slay the day no matter where you set up shop.

But just because you can work anywhere doesn't mean you should. And the same goes for brainstorming. Your spatial needs may change depending on your mood or the ideas you're after. Sometimes, brainstorming by yourself will lead to lots of ideas, while other times, situating yourself in the center of a crowded place will get the sparks flying. Sometimes movement might set ideas in motion, while other days you'll require a centering stillness.

The good news is brainstorming is quite possibly more flexible than where you choose to work, as most of the techniques you'll learn later in this book don't rely heavily on gadgets, technology, or Internet connections (You're welcome, data plans!). Still, it might take a few tries to play matchmaker with your creative challenge and the space best suited for discovering its solutions.

BRAINSTORMING BASE CAMP

Too many options can be overwhelming at times, so let's begin by setting up your brainstorming base camp. That might be your office, an area of your home, or somewhere in town—each of which we'll explore in depth in this section.

As Wonder Women, we don't have a shared office space, so we generate our ideas individually. But when we need to brainstorm together, we find it best to meet on neutral territory. That way, Carrie's snoring bulldog doesn't distract Jessica, and Jessica's Hot Wheels–loving son doesn't literally crash into our session.

We've brainstormed in all kinds of settings—sunk inside giant beanbags, laid out on cushy meeting room couches, sitting low on floor cushions in a Japanese-style tea room, shaded from the summer sun beneath lakeside trees. Sometimes we choose new spaces, and other times we pick old favorites. It's based on how we feel, what will make us most comfortable, what will get our minds moving in new ways—also who offers chocolate (the latter being top priority). Bottom line: the environment matters almost as much as the exercises.

SCALING THE SUMMIT

Base camp will be your brainstorming home filled with all the provisions you need, but the goal isn't to stay forever. Instead it's to establish a safe place to start your idea sessions. The more comfortable you get as a solostormer, the more you'll want to get out and explore the great big world of ideas that awaits.

By the end of this section, you'll have a better lay of the idea-generating landscape, including tips and techniques to help you navigate the pitfalls of certain spaces and make the most of your time in others. Before you know it, you'll be setting off on regular idea pilgrimages like the brainstorming vagabond you were born to be.

DESK DANGERS AHEAD

As commonplace as desks are for working, they are often riddled with brainstorming booby traps. How many desk danger zones can you spot lurking and ready to ambush your creativity?

Stuck? Turn the page to check your answers!

DESK DANGERS DIFFUSED

Without your knowing it, your desk is peppered with potential hazards just waiting to compromise your creativity. Here are the six areas to be on the lookout for when transforming your work space into an idea den.

#1: Shed some light. When you want bright ideas, dim the light on your brainstorming space. While natural sunlight can improve your mood, a darker space can help free you from your inhibitions.[2] Think of it sort of like romantic mood lighting. After all, a German study showed that dim lighting triggers "a risky, explorative processing style."[3] *Me-ow!*

#2: Make a mess. While a clean, organized desk may make it appear as though you've got adulting down to a science, actual science shows a bit more mess can lead to a lot more creativity. This might be surprising to learn, especially since it seems clearing clutter would allow for more brain space—vacancies where ideas can pop up. However, researchers have found that clearing the desk creates an atmosphere of conformity, which leads to strictly in-the-box thinking. Tidy-deskers do score high in charitable giving, healthy eating, and not littering, but when those do-gooders need good ideas, they'll need to make their way to the dark . . . er, messy side.[4]

#3: Bring the noise. Some of us need quiet in order to tackle our to-do lists, but for others, such silence can be deafening. Instead of concentration, isolation and lack of distraction can produce a bit of stir-craziness. This is why many solo thinkers camp out in coffee shops to get work done. The sounds of other people clicking away on keyboards and holding hushed conversations while mugs of brewed beans are poured and steamed creates just enough background noise to pump up your productivity. A study found adding a bit of ambient sound—70 decibels, to be precise—can boost your creativity.[6] To create the coffee shop scene right at your desk, loop ambient noise into your office with the help of apps and online music stations.

#4: Get back to nature. Walking outside in the fresh air and sunshine, surrounded by endless shades of green, can feel like walking into a rainforest of ideas. But even if you're confined to your desk, you can still welcome Mother Nature's brainstorming bounty by surrounding your space with plants and flowers. In addition to increased productivity, research shows that work space foliage leads to improved innovation and creative problem solving.[5]

#5: Pick a new perk. Coffee, in all its caffeinated glory, is quite often the fuel that powers the workday. It makes sense, as java not only jump-starts your brain but also fights fatigue, quickens your reaction time, improves your decision-making abilities, and ups your overall energy level. But before you pour that second mug, know that your cup o' Joe comes with a downside: caffeine can be a creativity killer. That's because caffeine stimulates your brain to be laser focused rather than open and malleable.[7] So when you're in need of ideas, back off on the beans before the brainstorming begins.

#6: Power down. Just about every parenting magazine recommends limiting kids' screen time in the name of health. But what about us grown-ups? A 2016 Nielsen report revealed that adults spend nearly 11 hours per day glued to screens of some sort.[8] While a big portion of that time—possibly 40 or more hours a week—is work related, we still spend a wealth of waking hours consuming digital media. Sure, being informed can help to inspire ideas, but the negative effects might outweigh the benefits. Maybe the most devastating negative effect? Loss of sleep.[9] Screens can worsen your Z's or cause you to lack sleep altogether. When you don't get enough sleep, various areas of your life and health suffer, and creative insight is one of them.[10] As you set the stage for brainstorming, don't forget to factor in bedtime. Cut the cord on screens once in a while, and get the rest you need in order to generate ideas during the day.

ANSWER TO PREVIOUS PAGE, CLOCKWISE: extremely tidy desk, coffee mug, closed notebook, computer screen on, unsharpened pencils, harsh lamp lighting, a dead plant, speakers switched off

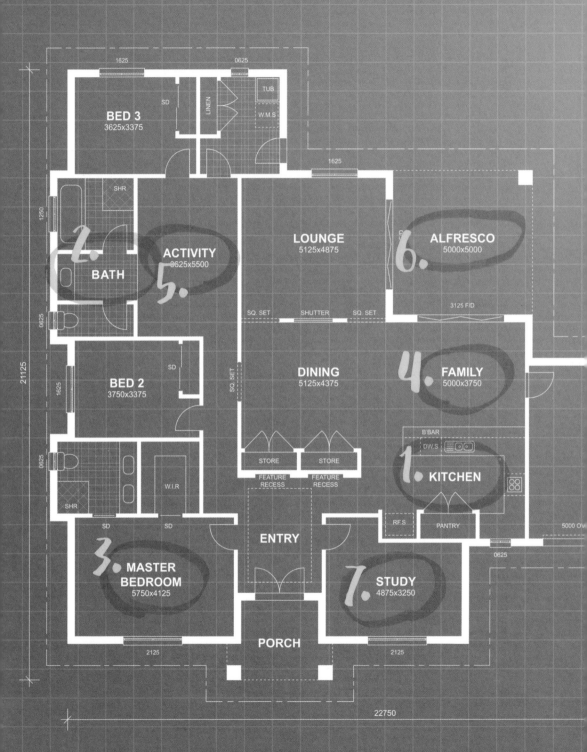

A FLOOR PLAN FULL OF IDEAS

Want inspiration at every turn? Zoom in to see how you can prep each room in your home for maximum idea potential.

#1. SPICE IT UP

Turn up the heat on creativity by digging into a variety of recipes and cuisines. Seek out new flavors and aromas—an unusual taste or unfamiliar smell just might spark your next big idea.

#2. SOAK IT IN

(See also #7 in our Ground Rules: "Take a Shower.") Let your brain stray as you suds up beneath the warmth of the water. Or better yet, enjoy a bubble bath and find yourself saturated with ideas.

#3. WRITE IT DOWN

Nothing stirs the mind quite like hitting the hay. Often, our best ideas occur to us just as we're headed to bed. Rather than let them keep you up all night, jot your thoughts in a bedside notebook. Or clear your mind by doing a bit of journaling before sleep.

#4. PLAY IT THROUGH

Take a break from the solo life and get social with family and friends. Connect with your inner child and explore toys, games, and other communal activities to see how they shift your perspective and inspire new methods of problem solving.

#5. WORK IT OUT

A sweat session isn't just about building heart health or a so-called bikini body; it can also boost your creativity. Research shows exercise can get your brain in shape to better tackle problems in innovative ways.[11] Think of your morning treadmill session as a bod-buffing brainstorm.

#6. FRESHEN IT UP

If plants and flowers in your office can encourage ideas to bloom, just imagine what your backyard could do. The great outdoors has been shown to enhance creativity, so nurture your connection to nature by daydreaming on your deck, digging in the dirt, or devoting yourself to yard duties.[12]

#7. READ IT THROUGH

Few activities can shift your perspective like reading a good book. Research reveals that reading can get your brain thinking in new ways—which is great for generating ideas.[13] At the same time, reading offers an escape from reality and exposes you to experiences you might never have thought were possible for you. So while chilling out with a book may seem like the opposite of work, it can help prime your brain for creative heavy lifting.

INTERIOR DESIGN FOR IDEAS

If creativity is at the heart of all good ideas, and home is where the heart is, then it only makes sense to design your space with creativity in mind. That doesn't mean you need to knock down walls, paint your office neon orange, or put an addition on the house—unless you want to, of course! Instead, look for little ways to welcome ideas into your space.

⦿ Get touchy-feely. When brainstorming, you're on the prowl for ideas that pop. For a space that does the same, skip scrutinizing paint swatches and head straight for texture. By texture, we don't just mean what's soft or rough to the touch. Texture also refers to visual interest, weight, and a sense of depth. Even the best-laid interior design plans can fall flat if texture is forgotten, so try a few of these tactile tips.

- Twist your textiles, mixing linens, flannels, cottons, faux furs, and tapestries to create dimension in throw pillows, blankets, window treatments, bedding, tablecloths, and upholstery.

- Create a natural texture in your space by decorating with potted plants, cacti, and flowers with differing sizes, weights, or growth patterns.

- Ground yourself with a layering of area rugs—bonus points for mixing prints!

- Instead of selecting a matching set of furniture, combine complementing patterns, textures, shapes, and materials for a cozier feel.

- Cover your walls in textured wallpaper, fabric, or an innovative paint technique.

Color me pine. Turns out Kermit was wrong: it *is* easy being green. A published study showed that yellow + blue = the best hue for inspiring creativity and ideas.[14] Scientists reason that the brain connects the color green with nature and growth, which motivates the mind to flourish. So try painting an accent wall artichoke, reupholstering an old sofa in sea green, or papering a bathroom with forest-inspired wallpaper.

Double down. Who says a bedroom is just for sleeping? Or a dining room just for eating? Not us! If you haven't already, you'll soon find that brainstorming isn't always about coming up with a completely new idea. Sometimes it's about repurposing an old one. Reflect this concept in your physical space (and save a bit of cash) by finding new ways to display or use what you already own.

- Loft a bed to add a desk, reading nook, or craft bar underneath.

- Decorate a wall with framed vintage mirrors to help a small space feel bigger.

- Give dual duty to storage cubes, using them as ottomans, step stools, seating, and side tables, all while they keep your odds and ends tucked away.

- Put everyday objects on display. Colorful colanders, wooden spoons, pretty plates, and beautiful baskets can all make interesting wall art.

OUT ON THE TOWN

Home may not be the brainstorming space for you, especially if you've got a clingy roommate or even clingier kids or have yet to build those fences that make good neighbors. Leaving your office can feel like slacking on the job, but as we take a tour of town, you'll discover all kinds of suitable spaces in which to set up your idea-building shop.

PUBLIC TRANSIT

Best for people-watching, local sightseeing, stress-free commuting, power naps, small-talk sessions, podcast listening.

COFFEE SHOP

Best for free Wi-Fi, ample seating, ambient noise, amazing aromas.

LIBRARY

Best for free Wi-Fi, extreme silence, avoiding small talk, tables on which to spread out your stuff, instant access to research materials, limited distractions.

WINDOW SHOPPING

Best for trend spotting, market research, pricing analysis, non-nature walking.

DOCTOR'S OFFICE

Best for people-watching, free magazines.

TRAILS

Best for surrendering to green space, seeing wildlife, exercising the body and mind, letting go of stress.

PARK

Best for enjoying nature, moving freely, breathing fresh air, feeling childlike.

MUSEUM

Best for art inspiration, educational exhibits, provoking questions, new perspectives, gentle movement, calming environment.

ECLECTIC NEIGHBORHOOD

Best for design ideas, aesthetic inspiration, community involvement, exposure to new local businesses, trend spotting.

RESTAURANT

Best for exploring new cuisines, trying different flavor combinations, people-watching, feeling less hangry.

BAR

Best for socializing with strangers, experiencing creative craft brews and mixers, chilling out.

GROCERY STORE

Best for real-world immersion, market research, color inspiration, advertising tactics, appealing produce.

FARMERS MARKET

Best for seasonal inspiration, local business owners networking, color palette creativity, casual walking, community learning.

GYM

Best for exercising the body and mind, enjoying relaxing spa services, taking classes, people-watching.

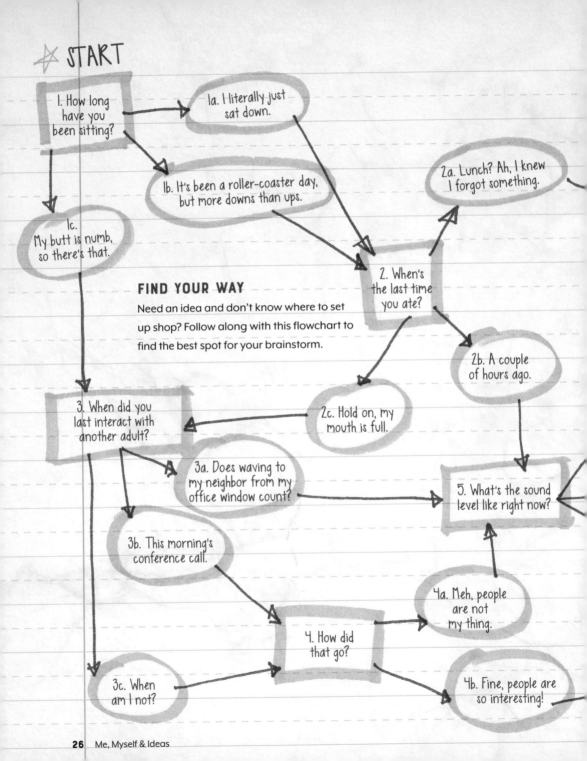

✶ START

1. How long have you been sitting?

1a. I literally just sat down.

1b. It's been a roller-coaster day, but more downs than ups.

1c. My butt is numb, so there's that.

2a. Lunch? Ah, I knew I forgot something.

FIND YOUR WAY

Need an idea and don't know where to set up shop? Follow along with this flowchart to find the best spot for your brainstorm.

2. When's the last time you ate?

2b. A couple of hours ago.

3. When did you last interact with another adult?

2c. Hold on, my mouth is full.

3a. Does waving to my neighbor from my office window count?

5. What's the sound level like right now?

3b. This morning's conference call.

4a. Meh, people are not my thing.

3c. When am I not?

4. How did that go?

4b. Fine, people are so interesting!

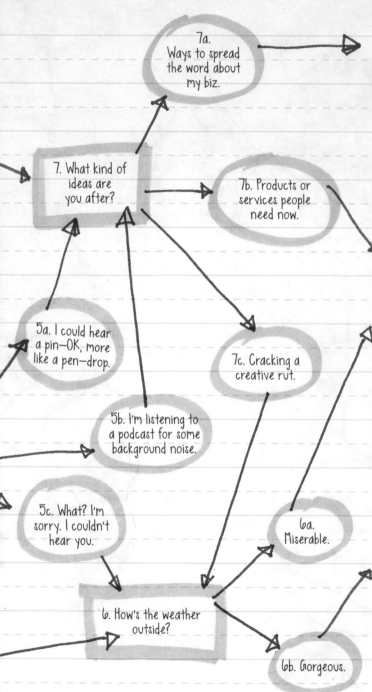

A: Social Scenes

Make a break for places where people congregate, including cafés, coffee shops, and bars. You don't have to break into small talk with every person you meet, but try becoming a watcher of the world. Observe your neighbors in their natural habitat for ideas about how people interact with others or occupy their alone time.

B: Where the Wares Are

Take a stroll through shops, galleries, and other artsy areas to study up on the latest trends. You don't need a dime to browse through places like boutiques, farmers markets, grocery stores, or malls to find color, design, product, and service inspiration to add to your small biz.

c: The Great Outdoors

Fresh air is just what you need to let your mind wander. Tackle a trail filled with foliage and fauna. If going green ain't your scene, walk it out in the hip neighborhoods that surround you. Even a walk around your own neighborhood could do a blocked brain a world of good.

7a. Ways to spread the word about my biz.

7. What kind of ideas are you after?

7b. Products or services people need now.

5a. I could hear a pin—OK, more like a pen—drop.

7c. Cracking a creative rut.

5b. I'm listening to a podcast for some background noise.

5c. What? I'm sorry. I couldn't hear you.

6a. Miserable.

6. How's the weather outside?

6b. Gorgeous.

A WORLD OF IDEAS

Your desk, home, and town are just a few places where ideas can flourish, but don't ignore the great big world around you. After all, if a simple change of cuisine can elevate your mind's eye, just imagine what immersing yourself in a foreign culture could do.

If this feels far-fetched, we hear ya! Dusting off the passport and jet-setting to new lands won't become the brainstorming trick you rely on often. Heck, maybe traveling is something you do only once every few years. But we can just about promise that making a break for a new place will pay off in ways to which ideating at your desk can't even remotely compare.

WHERE TO?

There are a lot of places to see out there, so narrowing down your choices might feel a bit cumbersome. Here are some tips to help point you in the right direction.

Budget: **TRAVELING AIN'T CHEAP.** If you're dreaming of yachts on seas near secluded islands but your bank account is more rowboat-on-the-local-pond, plan accordingly. Always base your adventure on what you can afford—unless you're skilled in mooching off others. Then the sky's the limit!

Bucket list: **WE'VE ALL GOT THOSE THINGS WE WANT TO DO BEFORE WE KICK THE SO-CALLED BUCKET.** If travel is on your list, then your destinations are probably mapped out for you. Time's not slowing down, so buy that airline ticket, book that hotel, and schedule that safari.

Mental state: **IN ADDITION TO OTHER COUNTRIES, YOU HAVE A FULL 50 STATES FROM WHICH TO SELECT.** But the one state that matters most is your mental state. That is, how do you want to feel? Want to spike your adrenaline? Journey toward thrill-seeking hot spots. Need to chillax? There's a beach chair and umbrella-adorned drink with your name on it. Want to connect with your inner child? Pack it up for a fun-filled amusement park. Ready to feel the wind in your hair on the open road? Get your road-tripping kicks on Route 66.

Event: **GET MORE BANG FOR YOUR TRAVELING BUCK BY BEING PURPOSEFUL ABOUT YOUR TRIP.** When a family reunion or old college pal's wedding calls you out of town, add on a few extra days for yourself to explore the surroundings. This is especially great if it's a place to which you'd normally never travel, as you're likely to experience the locale free of expectations.

Learn: **NO REUNIONS OR WEDDINGS ON THE BOOKS?** Find an event to attend. We suppose that could mean crashing a destination wedding, but a less criminal approach is to seek out conferences or retreats to boost your brain power. Whether it's for business, skill building, creativity, or pleasure, there's a conference (and likely at a cool place!) just waiting for you.

Spontaneity: **IF YOU LOVE A GOOD SURPRISE, FLY BY THE SEAT OF YOUR PANTS AND LET FATE BE YOUR TRAVEL AGENT.** Instead of planning, wait for your travel dates to pick up airfare at last-minute pricing or head to the airport to grab a seat on standby. You could also try letting a friend or family member select your destination. Or try a travel agency that plans a surprise trip for you.

BRAIN BREAK: A Space of Her Own

Finding just the right space in which to be your creative best can take time. For Jessica—the introverted half of the Wonder duo—it took a few pieces of wood, some curtains, and the courage to do things her own way.

Jessica especially loves her alone time. She works best when she can tackle her tasks in peace and quiet. When Jessica worked at American Girl, she adjusted to the cubicle life as best she could, but the going was rough. Sure, the open-office environment encouraged collaboration (and snack-sharing), but it offered no respite from noise and other distractions. Then, one day, a miracle arrived in the form of an e-mail announcement: employees were encouraged to get creative with their work spaces.

The idea person that she is, Jessica hatched a plan with her architect cousin to transform her plain, half-walled, personality-lacking cubicle into a tiki-hut-meets-IKEA dream space. For the sake of reading ease, let's call it the She-bicle. Jessica provided the dimensions and photos of the existing space to her cousin, and together they worked up a vision before he sketched out the plans. In the spirit of team building, Jessica called upon a woodworking coworker to build the structure that would become her creative den.

The She-bicle was awe-inspiring. In fact, it's part of what convinced Carrie to join the company when she toured the office shortly after. Though she hadn't yet met the She-bicle dweller, Carrie vowed to become her BFF. (Mission accomplished.)

3

ICE-BREAKERS

CHIP AWAY AT WORK MODE TO
EXPOSE YOUR INNER CREATIVITY.

AWESOME, NOT AWKWARD

ANOTHER BRAINSTORMING BENEFIT we failed to mention? Not feeling awkward! *(Unless you find being alone awkward. If so, you might want to give serious thought to the entrepreneurial career path you've chosen. Just sayin'.)*

In a traditional group brainstorm, after the introductions are made and seats are claimed, but before the actual ideating begins, there's that uncomfortable period during which you feel a bit like a bumbling idiot. Regardless of how well you know the other people in the room, self-consciousness can kick in and nerves may knock you down a peg as you gear up to prove to your boss and your peers what an absolute genius you are. Really, no pressure.

In a team setting, it's necessary to encourage everyone to relax and ditch the stress. Of course, that's easier said than done. It would be great if everyone could just flip the awkward switch to the "off" position and move calmly and coolly about the idea session. But if you've ever been on a bad first date, you know that's simply not possible.

ICE, ICEBREAKER

As a solution to such awkwardness, someone had this *brilliant* thought: "Hey, since chitchatting about the weather isn't a painful enough exercise in random, unnecessary communication, let's make everyone interact in completely unnatural ways." People cheered, hoisted this virtuoso on their shoulders, and thus, icebreakers came to be. (That's how we assume it went down anyway.)

Icebreakers are typically lighthearted activities designed to make everyone giggle, squirm, and cough nervously until the only obvious thing left to do is split BFF necklaces.

But the truth is that icebreakers tend to have the exact opposite effect. Really, how is it possible not to shudder at the thought of . . .

- holding hands in a circle to create a human knot (and then "problem solving" to untangle yourselves).

- a game of telephone in which someone (usually a complete stranger, most likely with coffee breath) whispers into your ear.

- passing a ball around the room as you call out your favorite fruit.

- conducting an interview with another person, and then attempting to remember everything that person said so that you can properly introduce them to the rest of the group (all while overcoming your fear of public speaking). You know, because remembering a person's name isn't hard enough.

You may think we're exaggerating, perhaps even making these examples up. The reality is that we've actually been forced to participate in these activities. There are plenty more where these came from, but we'll save them for our therapists.

JUST CHILL

The beauty of brainstorming solo is just that—you're all by yourself with no one but the bully in your mind to make you feel uncomfortable. That said, we're sorry to say that being on your own doesn't excuse you from having to break the ice. Your "ice" is just a little different in nature.

Instead of a thick barrier of awkwardness, mental focus is now the obstacle standing between you and big ideas. Another purpose of traditional icebreaker games is to help you transition from sitting quietly at your cube to sharing ideas in a group setting. Likewise, when you're ideating alone, you have to transition from sitting quietly at your desk to, well, sitting quietly at your desk. Which is harder than it sounds. It's just as difficult to flip the creative switch to the "on" position as it is to flip the awkward switch to the "off" position—especially after you've spent half the day in get-work-done mode.

This section is meant to send your brain on a little trip—away from what it's currently doing (for example, invoicing, e-mailing, stressing over looming deadlines, preparing estimates). Because if you're going to brainstorm effectively, you'll need to temporarily leave your to-dos behind.

LEARNER'S PERMIT

Throughout this section, think of us as your driving instructors back before you turned 16. As much as you would've loved to take your dad's cool car for a pleasure cruise around town, the state (and probably your parents) required you to obtain a license. And to do that, you had to understand the rules of the road.

Obviously, you don't need a license to brainstorm, but some of the same principles apply to ideating as to driving. In this section, we'll demonstrate how to operate your idea-generating vehicle (a.k.a. your brain) when your work mind is moving toward a head-on collision. Then, we'll set you up in simulators to help you learn to embrace the power of constraints. And finally, when you're ready to get behind the wheel, we'll offer hands-on exercises meant to power down the taskmaster side of your brain and provoke your creativity. When your training is complete, we'll hand you the keys to your very own, properly fueled idea engine.

Ready? Let's roll . . .

CHANGING LANES

The working mind operates much like a car on a multilane highway. As you merge from the on-ramp into traffic, it takes a moment to get up to speed. You stay in the right lane—the slow lane, if you will—as you find your bearings, achieve your pace, and get comfortable with the trip ahead. The "slow lane" of the workday might look like sipping your coffee while reviewing and responding to e-mails or creating a to-do list.

Once you're in the zone, you switch to the middle lane, where you can coast to your destination or, to continue with the metaphor, get work done at a steady pace. Sure, there will be distractions (billboards, rude drivers, hazards in the road), but for the most part, you can set your cruise control and travel in comfort.

Then there's the far left lane. We'll call this the "fast lane." Working in the fast lane is often necessary when you have deadlines, an overbooked calendar, or demanding clients who seem to need everything yesterday. It's a tricky and potentially risky place to be but a good option when you're in a pinch.

TAKE THE SCENIC ROUTE

The idea-generating mind can also be imagined as a motor vehicle, but while both mind-set types share a similar Point A, Point B and the route you take to get there are what set the thinking styles apart. Throughout the workday, you're likely to switch lanes multiple times, but typically the destination is always the same: finish your tasks. And it becomes such a common commute, no matter your speed, that it's easy to go on autopilot. That doesn't mean you skip paying attention to the road or driving defensively; rather, your mind simply is never put to the test of navigating new terrain.

Oftentimes we get behind the wheel of our to-do list and everyday agendas, which causes us to bypass the exits for brainstorming new ideas. Traveling new roads and breaking from routine are ultimately what help to incite creativity. So when new ideas are needed, you can't take the familiar everyday route but have to stray from the well-paved path on journeys toward new views.

DRIVING STYLE

You know the old adage about life being about the journey and not the destination? That's true of brainstorming, too. When generating ideas, it's best to focus less on the finish line and more on the road that gets you there. To do so may require changing how you operate your "vehicle."

Autobahn Autopilot: Your day is completely mapped out, and your brain is ready to travel at full speed. Nothing can stand in your way or cause you to take a detour.

 Even though staying focused is a good thing, with the pedal to the metal it's nearly impossible to see what interesting things pass you by. Downshift a gear and let your brain take in the ride.

Distracted Driver: Texting, talking on the phone, mapping out your tasks, or just scrolling for a favorite podcast is an entertaining way to fill the day. After all, why keep yourself busy when others can do it for you?

 While distractions can lead to curiosity, and curiosity can lead to ideas, avoid falling down the rabbit hole. We all know that texting while driving—however innocent it may feel in the moment—can spell disaster. Likewise, a text volley or trip online to check a friend's feed can bust a brainstorm before it starts. As you move toward your final destination, remember to keep your eye on the prize.

Sunday Driver: Ah! Nothing like a day of driving along the coastal highway of creativity with no map in hand. Right, left, north, south—all directions lead to Easy Street!

Having a relaxed, expectation-free approach to brainstorming is great, but avoid checking out completely. Brainstorming comes with a certain level of freedom, but as you steer away from deadlines and to-do lists, don't drift too far toward unproductiveness.

Stuck in Traffic: You see the sign: Ideas Ahead! Then suddenly orange cones and slow-moving traffic cause a no-budge roadblock in your brain.

Creativity can come to a brake-screeching halt if you can't step away from your work. Instead of forcing your brain to get on board, give in a little. When you're in a traffic jam, no amount of complaining or mental willing can give you the green light you want. When it comes to creativity, a mental block can work the same way. While traffic is slow, take care of one or two smaller tasks on your to-do list. A sense of accomplishment and progress may be all you need in order to move forward creatively.

Mom Taxi: When you're a parent, your vehicle may be registered to you, but it's the soccer practices, dance recitals, PTA meetings, grocery trips, and pediatric visits that ultimately dictate your course.

Other people's needs are important, but don't forget who's the boss. (Hint: You.) Spending your mental energy on everyone else will only leave you exhausted, overwhelmed, and, quite possibly, regretting your decision to go solo. Creativity will require "me" time, so while you set about your day addressing everyone else's needs, don't forget to pencil in time for yourself.

REJECT THE JOYRIDE

It's true that brainstorming is best when the weight of the world isn't crushing your spirit, but too much freedom and you might actually get nowhere.

Research shows constraints, or limitations and obstacles, are actually better for innovation than unbridled freedom.[1] If you're struggling with this concept, you may be thinking of constraints as barriers. Instead, look at them as opportunities.

A CRASH COURSE IN CONTROLLED CREATIVITY

In one study participants were examined to see how creatively they used their resources when influenced by scarcity versus abundance.[2] When participants were given an abundance of resources, they had little incentive to be innovative. Why think outside the box when the box is filled with everything you'll ever need? However, when participants were given scarce resources, they were motivated to innovate.

Constraints provide perspective and focus, clearly shaping the challenge that exists. They force you to stretch your imagination and get your wheels turning in unexpected ways. When time, money, or resources are scarce, be prepared for creativity to swell.

For practice, try applying constraints to your everyday life.

- What would you make for dinner if you *only had four ingredients* to work with?

- What would you wear to a client meeting if you had to *wear only blue*?

- How would you *replace your wall art* using only items you already own?

- How would you entertain yourself if you *didn't have a TV*, computer, tablet, or phone?

After just one attempt, you might find that these limitations lead you to a new recipe, an outfit you never considered, innovative decor, or a board game you forgot you loved to play.

Possibly the last place you want to end up when brainstorming ideas is a dead end. The quickest way to get there? Indulging any or all of these common fears:

- **fear of rejection**
- **fear of failure**
- **fear of embarrassment**
- **fear of not knowing where or how to begin**
- **fear of not being good enough**
- **fear of not having enough time**

Fear keeps you in your comfort zone. Sometimes, your comfort zone is the hippest scene in town. It provides a lot of what makes your brain and body feel good: minimal stress, a controlled environment, lowered levels of anxiety, and increased happiness, not to mention your favorite yummy treats like chips and dip with a side of wine.

Take Sunday lounging, for example. While you're all cozy on the couch, a friend texts you to join her for a run. Since you've barely been vertical in the last 24 . . . er, yikes, make that 48 hours, you know the fresh air and exercise could offer the renewed energy and optimism you need as motivation to clean the house, work on a home project, run errands, pay your bills, or heck, just take a shower.

Then you remember your running-partner friend is training for a half marathon, while you tend to get winded just lacing up your sneakers. You immediately start to worry she'll run too quickly or too far and you won't be able to keep up. You'll be embarrassed if she has to slow down and walk with you instead of getting in the training she needs. Suddenly, you couldn't care less that some exercise might lead to a better mood and increased productivity; your couch is safe, and that's where you choose to stay.

CONSTRUCTION ZONE

Feeling safe is important. But if you want to boost creativity, safe is not the way to go. Instead, stretch your comfort zone—do things you enjoy, but add a little risk and unknown to the equation. That way, you'll explore and troubleshoot, rather than follow a series of familiar steps.

That said, the goal isn't to push yourself so far that you end up panicked. Instead, take baby steps. For example, if you like to doodle, switch up your medium. Instead of the safety of a pencil and eraser, go for a more permanent pen or marker and see where your creativity leads. If you make a mistake, let it serve as inspiration to take your drawing down a reimagined route.

LET CREATIVITY TAKE THE WHEEL

When transitioning from working mode to idea-generating mode, be prepared for your brain to approach the "task" of creativity in the same manner it does everyday work tasks. You may find yourself striving for any or all of the following:

- perfection
- efficiency
- speed
- discipline

- skill
- a plan
- focus
- the answer

These are things your brain has been trained to go after, so it's perfectly natural for your mind to slip into this gear when presented with any task. But idea generating requires a less aggressive approach. Instead of speed and focus, you'll need to cultivate the following:

- childlike whimsy
- a leisurely pace
- adventurousness
- openness to imagination

- curiosity
- openness to inspiration
- playfulness
- not coming to a conclusion

Don't worry if this sounds next to impossible. The activities on the following pages are designed to help you step out of your comfort zone and power your innovative instincts into overdrive. The exercises are divided into the following categories:

Child's Play: RELIVE YOUR YOUTH.

Make It New: THINK LIKE A GENIUS.

Find Your Own Hemingway: WRITE? RIGHT.

Mirror, Mirror: GET TO KNOW YOU EVEN BETTER.

Blue Sky: BECAUSE ANYTHING IS POSSIBLE.

TIME CRUNCH

If you're pressed for time, you may be inclined to skip these "silly brain-benders" (your words, not ours). But because each of these exercises is designed to prime your brain for ideal ideating, we hope you'll invest a little blind faith in this minor, but still important, step of the process.

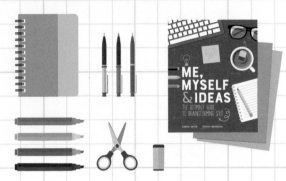

WHAT YOU'LL NEED:

- a blank notebook or blank sheets of paper
- pen and pencil
- this book
- magazines
- glue stick
- scissors
- your favorite markers

BRAINSTORMING BIN

Whether you have two minutes or two hours, you can save yourself time by always having these supplies at the ready. Consider dedicating a bin to these materials so they're available to you at a moment's notice. Your Brainstorming Bin is also a great place to store this book!

It's time to rev up those creative engines!

Child's Play

Think back to your early elementary school years. There was a lot of cutting, pasting, and coloring and very few burdens or opinions. It was easy to spend an hour, if not all day, doing nothing but creating a farm landscape out of construction paper (the kind only your mother could love). The Child's Play activities are meant to take you right back to kindergarten, when you didn't have an inner (or outer) critic. They don't require logical thinking. In fact, the less you think, the better. Just do your best to let go of your inhibitions as you clear your mind's clutter to make room for intuitive creativity.

DEEP DIVE

Create an underwater scene using scissors and glue, and magazines, catalogs, or grocery mailers destined for the trash. Set a timer for what your schedule will allow, but cap your craft session at 20 minutes to start practicing some constraint.

SHOUT OUT TO ART

Draw one or more of the following sounds.

- BAM
- WAAAAH
- WHOA
- YAY
- CREEEAK
- POW

MOD ART

Scribble on a piece of paper like a toddler would. Grab a box of crayons or markers and fill in the shapes. It may not be gallery-worthy, but it will get your mind into creativity mode.

UP YOUR NAME GAME

Write your name in really fancy script—backward.

OLD-SCHOOL GYM CLASS

The easiest and fastest way to recharge those creative batteries is to move. So let's do it like you did back when recess was the best part of the day. Push yourself around on your wheeled office chair for 15 seconds, run in place for 30 seconds, do five jumping jacks, do three push-ups, and finish with five sit-ups. For bonus points, re-create the square-dancing unit everyone dreaded—this time, without the sweaty-palmed partner!

ONE-LINE DRAWING

Place a 3-D object in front of you. Without looking at your paper or lifting your pen, draw the object in one continuous line. Repeat a few times before hanging your drawing on the fridge for all to admire.

ROCK, PAPER, SCISSORS . . . WATERMELON?

Take the game of Rock, Paper, Scissors to the next level. Quickly conceive of a fourth object to add to the game. How would you represent it with your hand, and how could it defeat two of the other elements but lose to the third?

FEEL IT OUT

Using a pencil (not colored pencils!) draw a visual representation of one or more of the emotions listed below. Challenge yourself to go beyond facial expressions and explore what objects or scenes could stand in for these sentiments.

- mad
- joyous
- content

- giddy
- frightened
- jealous

- crazy
- surprised
- excited

Make It New

Innovation isn't always about creating from scratch. Sometimes, it's about seeing something ordinary in an extraordinary way. The following exercises challenge you to "make it new" by treating the familiar with a touch of the strange.

TWIST, DON'T SHOUT

You know the pile of twist ties at the base of your junk drawer? Bend and shape them into as many tiny sculptures as you can in five minutes or less. Now pretend your little works of art represent real products in miniature form. Imagine how each could be used in a variety of contexts:

- bakery
- hospital
- library
- school
- gym
- amusement park
- zoo
- laboratory
- city square

STIR IT UP

In your kitchen, randomly select a cooking utensil. Set a timer for one minute as you write down 20 ways in which this apparatus could be applied beyond its intended use.

(R)EVOLUTION

If dinosaurs and mastodons once roamed the earth, imagine what sorts of animals might exist in eras to come. Create a creature of the future by choosing one animal from each column and combining them to form a single critter. Draw it. Name it. Describe it. What does it do? What does it eat? Can it be a pet? Is it helpful to humanity?

alligator	kitten
parrot	rhinoceros
mouse	turtle
chimpanzee	owl
octopus	clown fish
kangaroo	camel
chameleon	bulldog
horse	platypus
koala	llama

CURIOSITREE

Create a family tree for an inanimate object, filling its branches with related objects of the past, present, and future. As an example, we gave roots and branches to our favorite food-storing appliance—the refrigerator.

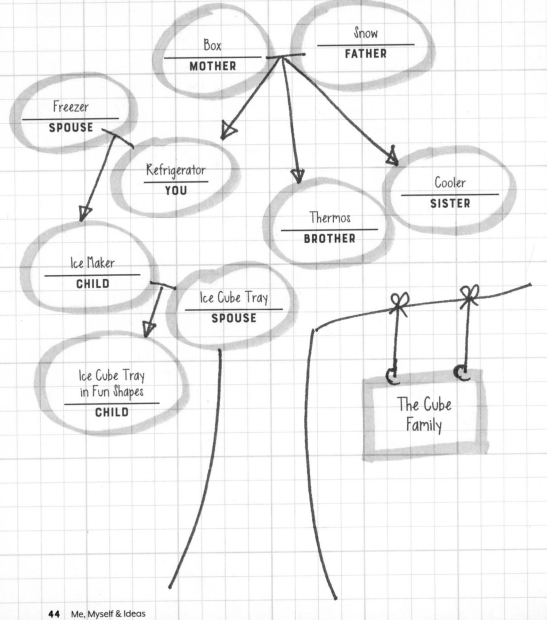

Box
MOTHER

Snow
FATHER

Freezer
SPOUSE

Refrigerator
YOU

Thermos
BROTHER

Cooler
SISTER

Ice Maker
CHILD

Ice Cube Tray
SPOUSE

Ice Cube Tray
in Fun Shapes
CHILD

The Cube
Family

Find Your Own Hemingway

Before you utter the words "I can't write," remember that stepping out of your comfort zone—even just a baby step beyond the boundary—can reap big rewards for your future ideas. We're not expecting the next great American novel—or even the next mediocre American novel. The goal here is to use writing to free your mind and lift any barriers standing in the way of your creativity.

IN THREE WORDS

Write movie descriptions for the following movies using only three words:

- E.T.
- Pretty Woman
- The Lion King
- Titanic
- The Sound of Music
- Frosty the Snowman

LAUGHABLE LINES

It's time to rhyme. Close your eyes and spin around in your chair (or stand and spin in place a few times, if your chair isn't a swivel). When you open your eyes, note the very first thing you see; this will be the subject of your verse. Give yourself two minutes to write a silly, rhyming poem. Put on a mock performance for an imaginary poetry slam audience, or add some beats and rap the words.

BINGEWORTHY

Open any book to a random page and plop your finger down without looking. Write down the word to which you've pointed. Repeat this exercise two more times on different pages in the book until you have three words. Create a synopsis of a new TV series using those three words.

VACATIONS PERSONIFIED

Using the prompt below, fill in the blank on the left with the name of a person you know or a favorite celebrity. Fill in the blank on the right with a vacation destination that fits his or her personality. Repeat the exercise until you run out of names.

IF _____ WERE A VACATION, HE/SHE WOULD BE _____.

BRAIN NAVIGATOR

Choose one of the following objects. Set a timer for one minute and let your stream of consciousness flow as you write down every word or thought your brain associates with your selection. Repeat the exercise with a second object and a third.

- a waterbed
- a half-eaten hamburger
- a librarian's glasses
- sweaty shoes
- a crumpled piece of paper
- a wine cork
- a dress on a clothesline
- a paper-towel dispenser
- a sandbox
- a pinball machine

A SANDBOX

sand
bucket
castle
king
queen
chess
game
sports
athlete
strong
muscle
anatomy
science
experiment

FOUR SCORE AND . . .

Innovation has come a long way over the years, and what is possible today would likely boggle the minds of our ancestors. Write down how you would explain the following modern conveniences to your great-great-great-grandmother/father.

- online shopping
- dating apps
- media streaming
- smartphones
- space flight
- coffee shops

Mirror, Mirror

You got to know your inner brainstormer a bit better in Section One, but it's time to dig a little deeper.

YOU, ONLY YOUNGER

Quiz your 8-year-old self with the following questions. How would he or she respond?

- **What are your best qualities?**
- **What is your favorite class in school?**
- **What do you do when you get home from school?**
- **What do you want to be when you grow up?**
- **What is your idea of a perfect day?**

Now ask the same questions of your 18-year-old self.

NOW & THEN

Make a list of 10 things you have in common with your 8-year-old self. Then make a list of 10 things you hope to have in common with your 80-year-old self. Compare the two lists to see where the younger and older versions of you merge.

DEAR FEAR

Write a letter to something that truly terrifies you. Maybe it's an actual thing or maybe it's an emotion or situation. Then write your fear's response to you. What did it tell you? Are you less or more afraid of it, having read its reply?

GET UP AND VAN GOGH

Whether you're a trained artist or all thumbs, you know what tasks will test your sketching skills. Embrace the discomfort and choose your drawing challenge. If you know you "can't draw people," draw some people. If a particular drawing style gives you trouble (think photo-realism, caricature, anime, gestural), select an object and sketch it with that technique in mind. To take the test to the next level, close your eyes and draw one of the following:

- **Statue of Liberty**
- **artichoke**
- **seashell**
- **tractor**
- **tube of toothpaste**
- **hot-air balloon**
- **lightbulb**
- **rose**
- **crown**
- **baseball**

JUST BECAUSE

Design a greeting card you'd like to receive right at this moment. Then design a card to give to yourself in 20 years.

JACKPOT!

Imagine you just won $100,000. What would you do with that money? Next, imagine what your 8-year-old self would do with the dough. How about your 18-year-old self?

THE ULTIMATE SELFIE

Design a billboard all about you. Remember that passing drivers only have a few seconds in which to absorb what they see. Think about what you're selling (a service, a character trait, among others). Who's your target audience, and how are you going to catch their attention and leave them wanting more?

Blue Sky

While we know constraints can boost creativity, now is your chance to throw limitation to the wind. In this section, there's no one saying, "Sorry, there's not enough money in the budget for that." This final batch of icebreakers is all about making dreams come true.

THE WILDEST WISH LIST EVER

Imagine you have access to a wish-granting genie. The catch? He'll only grant those wishes that are truly outlandish. Think: Impossible stuff. Set a timer for two minutes and write down as many worthy wishes as you can.

MOST LIKELY TO . . .

Write down the names of as many elementary school classmates as you can remember (and if your memory's a little rusty, go with middle school, high school, or even college peers). Pretend you're the owner of a big business and assign a job to each person as you see fit.

SPICE IT UP!

Pay a little visit to your spice cabinet. Close your eyes and randomly choose a container before carefully opening it and taking a (gentle) whiff. Repeat this two more times until you have selected three spices. If you were to create a blend of these three to package and sell, what would it be called? How would you describe it?

ACCENT-UATE

Get silly with yourself, reading headlines from the newspaper or a magazine using . . .

- the voice of a condescending boss.
- the voice of your favorite actor.
- the voice of a Southern belle.
- the voice of your best friend.
- the sounds an alien might use.

THE GIFT THAT KEEPS ON GIVING

Sometimes being resourceful means regifting. Scan your surroundings and select objects you could wrap and give to the following celebrities and historical figures. What would you choose to give, and how would each person benefit from your repurposed generosity?

- William Shakespeare
- Marie Curie
- Barack Obama
- Beyoncé

- Mother Teresa
- Bill Gates
- Alfred Hitchcock
- Kanye West
- Coco Chanel

- Babe Ruth
- Michael Jordan
- J. K. Rowling

MAP IT OUT

Visualizing the road ahead can help you better understand how best to reach your destination. Taking a literal approach to this concept, see how well you can navigate from memory. Draw a map from your current location to one of the following places:

- the dream house you'd buy if money were no obstacle
- the bar in town that serves the best margarita
- the park you played in as a child
- the place where you had your first kiss
- the home where you always feel welcome
- the clothing store you wish was your own personal closet
- the local bakery with the yummiest treats

Congrats! You've completed the '80s-movie training-montage portion of the book. You know what we mean—the part where Rocky Balboa slugs slabs of meat, does sweaty single-arm push-ups, and charges up the steps of the Philadelphia Museum of Art to the tune of a motivational anthem. No more meat-slugging for you—you've proven you're ready to brainstorm. But first, a short break.

BRAIN BREAK: *Thinking Outside the Box*

Have you ever wondered about the origin of the phrase "think outside the box"? Thinking happens in your brain, not a box. And that brain is stored inside your head, which is also not a box. Perhaps the box is your cubicle? Or the oversized appliance box you fear could become your home should this solopreneur thing not pan out?

It turns out the box goes back to the early 1970s when psychologist J. P. Guilford conducted a study on creativity, testing participants with nothing but a nine-dot puzzle and a pencil.

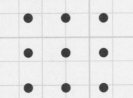

Each subject was challenged to connect all nine dots using four straight lines and without lifting their pencil from the paper. Although they were given no other rules, 80 percent of the participants viewed white space surrounding the box as a no-trespassing zone. The other 20 percent saw no boundaries and took their lines . . . wait for it . . . outside the box, thus solving the challenge in a couple of different ways.

Even though we told you the trick, see if you can find the solution without consulting the answer on page 124.

4 BRAINSTORM

THE STAGE IS SET, YOU'RE ALL WARMED UP, AND YOU KNOW THE RULES OF THE GAME.

get ready to blow your mind!

BACK TO SCHOOL

THERE ARE MANY WAYS to arrive at a given solution and many solutions to a given problem. We encourage you to get out and consider them all. To help, we've divided our brainstorming techniques into categories you're probably familiar with—school subjects. (Don't worry—there won't be any pop quizzes.) These handy icons will appear at the start of each brainstorming technique.

English

Forget analyzing plot structures, and think of "English" as playing with words. Use this category of techniques to write the way to your next big idea.

Art

You needn't know any art history or be a master painter to excel in this area. The ability to doodle, or just move a pen on paper, is the only requirement. The point is to employ your mind's eye to see the ideas that are likely staring you right in the face.

Drama

"To be, or not to be . . . " is actually not the question. Nor is it the start of a soliloquy you need to memorize, rehearse, and perform in front of an audience full of strangers. Heck, we've ditched the scripts, sets, and stage altogether. Instead, it's time to get into character and learn to view the world through the eyes of others.

Science

We have the likes of Einstein, Curie, Tesla, and Newton to thank for a few of our modern conveniences. However, following in their idea-genius footsteps won't require solving for x, understanding bases and acids, or learning how to use a Bunsen burner. Rather, this section is all about the hypothesis—that is, the educated guess from which further investigation follows. This scientific approach requires you to make assumptions, be curious, dig deeper, and question everything.

BRIGHT IDEAS

If you feel in the dark about how to apply a particular brainstorming exercise to your unique situation, look to the light. This light bulb accompanies case studies and application examples that might help you find your way.

HEED HAZARDS AHEAD

CONGRATS! YOU'RE ALL warmed up and ready to create. Before you jump in, prepare yourself for a few common brainstorming hazards.

POTENTIAL HAZARD: SLOW START

The start to most brainstorming sessions is slooooow. In those early moments, it's easy to get spooked and want to abandon the exercise altogether. Our advice is simple: *Keep going!*

- Keep going when brainstorming feels like the world's worst moment of awkward silence ever.

- Keep going when you feel stuck and begin questioning your very existence on this planet.

- Keep going when your brain begs of you to do absolutely anything else—especially when that something else is scrubbing toilets or scouring bathtubs. When bathroom chores begin to sound enticing, you'll know it's time to snap out of it.

- Keep going when "pretty good" is how you might describe the few ideas you've casually jotted down.

- Keep going when you hit a genius zone and the ideas are flying so fast you can barely capture them all.

- Keep going when you've reached the pivotal "aha" moment that causes you to start fantasizing about how you'll spend your newly amassed pile of riches.

Think the "aha" moment is where it ends? Nope. Sometimes that's merely the beginning. But you won't know until you've given your brain a chance to prove itself. Instead of letting your gut decide when to shut down the idea session, take a more pragmatic approach and set a measurable goal. That goal could be a quantity of ideas, a duration of time, or, heck, even a number of gray hairs sprouted. Then, once you've reached your goal . . .

Keep going! (SEE WHAT WE DID THERE?)

Like those torture-wielding personal trainers who say you've got five reps left, only to add five more, we've got your best interests in mind. You may not have buns of steel when you're done with our training, but your brain will be ready for some serious heavy lifting!

POTENTIAL HAZARD: DISTRACTIONS

Time-wasting tempters are going to try to draw away from your objective, even if you're on an idea roll. No matter how well the brainstorm is going, you can't stop the world from spinning. Instead of chasing after every squirrel that appears on your mental horizon, do your best to stay focused using these tips.

REMEMBER BRAINSTORMING RULE #1: UNPLUG. Power down the computer, close the laptop, and set your phone and tablet to silent. Even the tiny audible "ping" can be enough to hamper your momentum. E-mails, texts, notifications, and voice mails will all be waiting for you when your brainstorm session has concluded.

CHECK IN WITH YOURSELF. Disturbances aren't always external. Take a moment to assess what's going on in that head of yours. Write it all down. Now that it's been safely documented, you can get back to brainstorming, knowing you'll deal with what's bugging you later.

MAP THE WAY. Put a clear plan in place for your brainstorm session so that you know when you'll begin, what techniques you'll try, what goal you'll want to achieve, and how you'll react to the unexpected. Plotting your route helps remind you that you're moving forward instead of just walking in circles.

POTENTIAL HAZARD: BURNOUT

You are not a machine. Sometimes your brain and body just need a break. Follow these tips to help take care of you.

FUEL UP. It sounds basic, but a surprising number of people try to run on empty. If you're hungry, eat. If you're dehydrated, drink. If you're exhausted, sleep. Listen to your body, and give it what it needs.

SLOW DOWN. Speeding through your brainstorm can cause you to lose sight of the road and careen into a ditch. Give your mind the time it needs to find its way to a creative solution. This is not a race.

STOP. Some days just aren't meant for creativity. It's OK to give yourself a pass when you're just not feeling it. However, if this becomes a pattern, go back to the icebreakers and see if you can't break the spell.

ASSIGNMENT:

BUCKET LIST

English

TOOLS: Pen/pencil, paper, thesaurus

SUCH LISTS ARE no longer just for keeping tabs on the things you want to do and see before you kick the proverbial bucket. They're also for playing with words as a way of brainstorming names, titles, tasks, and more.

HOW TO:

1. Grab your paper and a pen. Draw three buckets (or boxes if you're not feeling very artistic today).

2. What are you stuck on? Quick: Think of three (or more!) words that describe your answer. Label each bucket with one word.

3. Now let the thesaurus do the work. Fill the buckets with as many words that mean something similar to the label as you can.

4. Once your buckets are full, empty the buckets and match the words together. Pair them up. Create phrases. Let the combos inspire new buckets.

5. There are more than 470,000 words in the English language.[1] But guess what? You're not limited to your native tongue! What words from other languages inspire you? Add those to the mix. *Voilà!*

NO NAME

This technique is perfect for naming businesses, menu items, products, events, or even your offspring, but don't limit yourself to those applications. Word pairing can inspire party themes, brand positioning, advertising campaigns, and more.

CASE STUDY: A gourmet dessert purveyor needs a name for her small business, which serves up sweet frozen treats.

FROZEN	TREAT	PLACE
cold	sugar	shoppe
brr	sweet	store
icy	dessert	shack
igloo	lolly	nest
ice cube	goodie	bar
frosty	delight	lounge
frigid	dolce	cabana
cool	pop	room
crisp	bonbon	suite
chilly	candy	hangout

BRR + BAR   DOLCE + CABANA   POP + SHOPPE

LOLLY + LOUNGE   BAR + BONBONS   SUGAR + SHACK

NOT YOUR MAMA'S MIND MAP

Art

TOOLS: Markers or colored pencils and a big sheet of paper

WE'VE ALL SEEN the basic mind map. You know the one:

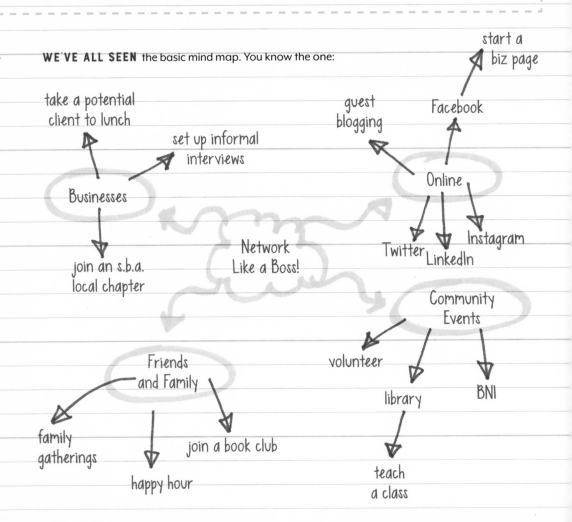

take a potential client to lunch

set up informal interviews

Businesses

join an s.b.a. local chapter

guest blogging

Facebook

start a biz page

Online

Twitter   Instagram

LinkedIn

Network Like a Boss!

Community Events

volunteer

library

BNI

Friends and Family

family gatherings

happy hour

join a book club

teach a class

Basic is great when it comes to fashion (for example, that one pair of black yoga pants that goes with everything), but it can get a little boring in the brainstorming world. So we've put our own special twist on this ideation classic.

Our version combines two of our favorite things: getting out of the office and people-watching. This activity works best in a public space where there are people aplenty. We're going to focus on a coffee shop, because coffee is the great unifier and you'll want as diverse a crowd as possible for this activity.

Off the beans? No worries. You can try this technique at a library, restaurant, coworking space, on mass transit, or really in any group setting where you need to look like you're paying attention but are actually bored beyond belief.

A PERKED-UP MIND MAP

Imagine your sheet of paper represents the coffee shop (or library or coworking space) where you're camped out. Start your mind map by drawing your table at its rough position in the room. Don't worry about being exact! Inside your table, write down your objective. Are you revamping your marketing approach? Attempting to solve a client problem? Looking for fashion trends to inspire your new website's color palette?

Now look around the room. Observe the people sitting at each table. How would you market to them? What media might they consume? How do you imagine they would approach the problem you need to solve? What are they wearing, doing, or talking about (eavesdropping strongly encouraged!) that might help you better understand their needs, desires, and tastes?

Draw the other tables in the room on your map and connect them to your own table with the traditional mind-mapping arrows. Label each table with a description of the person or people sitting there, and list your observations and insights below.

As you continue to observe, create branches extending from each table and more branches extending from those. [NOTE: Yes, since you're just observing, you'll be making all sorts of assumptions. But this activity isn't about accuracy; it's about borrowing other perspectives (even if those perspectives are totally imagined). The goal is to get outside your own head!]

CASE STUDY: *See a sample on the next page!*

magazines
posts on Facebook
nightly news
phone calls from friends
friends at book clubs

HOW THEY GET INFO

Three women in their
late 50s discussing
grown children
and husbands

Pitch myself as an expert
for magazine articles.

Design relevant memes for
this age group to repost.

Send direct-mail postcards.

Offer to speak before
book club meetings.

POSSIBLE MARKETING
OPTIONS

ME

NEW
MARKETING APPROACH
FOR MY BLOG

e-mail
Facebook/Instagram
other families
podcasts

HOW THEY GET INFO

Create advertisements
or content for school
newsletters.

Sponsor a family-
friendly event.

Partner with community
influencers (for example,
PTA members).

Mail out coupons for
"kids-eat-free" restaurants.

POSSIBLE MARKETING
OPTIONS

Family of five grabbing
a snack between
Saturday soccer games

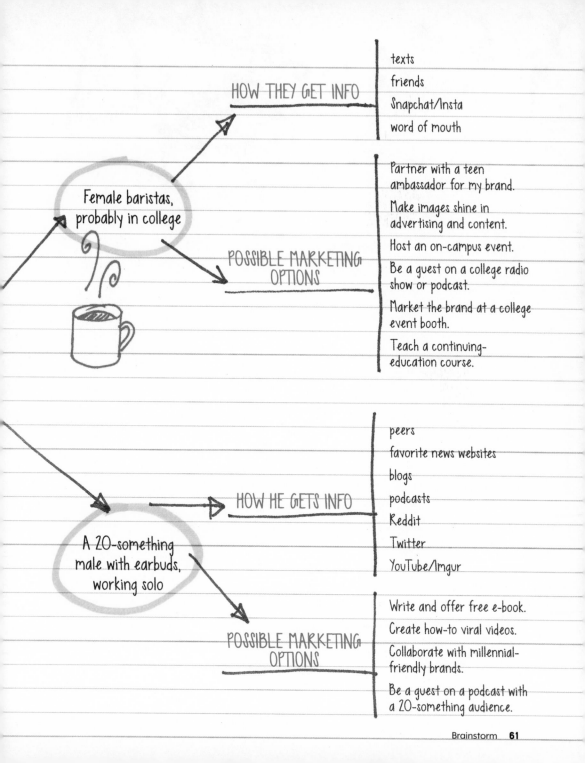

HOW THEY GET INFO

texts
friends
Snapchat/Insta
word of mouth

Female baristas, probably in college

POSSIBLE MARKETING OPTIONS

Partner with a teen ambassador for my brand.

Make images shine in advertising and content.

Host an on-campus event.

Be a guest on a college radio show or podcast.

Market the brand at a college event booth.

Teach a continuing-education course.

HOW HE GETS INFO

peers
favorite news websites
blogs
podcasts
Reddit
Twitter
YouTube/Imgur

A 20-something male with earbuds, working solo

POSSIBLE MARKETING OPTIONS

Write and offer free e-book.

Create how-to viral videos.

Collaborate with millennial-friendly brands.

Be a guest on a podcast with a 20-something audience.

AVATAR INVASION

Drama

TOOLS: Old magazines and catalogs, scissors, a glue stick, a large sheet of paper, pens/markers (optional)

NOPE, WE AREN'T referring to the blue-hued aliens of Pandora. In business-speak, your avatar is your perfect client, your ideal customer.

If you've been hustling to bring in any and all patrons just to pay the bills or have had a bad run of hellish customers, you might think "perfect clients" are about as science fiction as aliens. The truth is, they're out there—perfect clients, that is.

WHAT DO THEY LOOK LIKE?

To bring your avatar to life, you will need to be very specific about what "ideal" means to you. Start by filling in some basic details, including:

- gender
- age
- marital status
- number of children
- where they live
- occupation
- education

Once you've established the basics, the real fun can begin. Remember that the goal isn't to whip up a new species but to identify the habits, tastes, and needs of your avatar to help you better market or design your products or services. Look beyond basics like age and gender, and think about the following:

- stressors
- hobbies
- wardrobe
- design preferences
- vacation destinations
- idols
- goals
- news sources
- sexuality
- transportation
- politics
- social media
- health
- personality
- entertainment (movies, music, books, TV shows, podcasts, blogs)

APPLY IT: MAKE THEM MULTIPLY

Having a hard time identifying just one ideal customer? It's probably because you have more than one. Let's say you're a personal chef. An obvious avatar might be a busy single mom who needs help providing healthy meals for her kids. But single moms don't have a monopoly on busyness, health-consciousness, or the desire for delicious food. There are lots of people who tend to hold these traits and, thus, qualify as additional avatars: college students, seniors living alone, and two-parent families with jam-packed schedules. So after you create one avatar, think about who else might share their needs and tastes.

ASSEMBLE YOUR AVATARS

To design the clientele of your dreams, it's time to get a little crafty with collage. Sure, you could just make written lists of each avatar's character traits and interests and call it day. But where's the arts-and-crafts challenge in that?

Clip images from magazines and old catalogs to create collages that represent each avatar. The deeper you dig into each avatar's persona, the better you'll be able to tailor your brand, products, and content to their interests. They may only exist on construction paper for now, but you'll be surprised at how the work of rendering your avatars helps you land them as actual clients.

IDENTITY CRISIS

Business marketing not what you're after? This activity is also great for getting into the minds of your readers or audience and creating fictional characters for that book, movie script, or short story you're raring to write.

ASSIGNMENT:

BRAIN BLITZ

Science

TOOLS: A voice recorder and a stopwatch (both available as smartphone apps) and a pen/pencil and paper

THINK OF THIS brainstorming technique like speed dating, only instead of suitors, you're interviewing yourself.

HOW TO:

Set a stopwatch to create repeat rounds of 25 seconds. Choose 10 questions at random from our list. Record yourself as you answer each question lickety-split in the given time. Don't think, just respond.

After you've answered your 10 questions, it's time for a break. Set your stopwatch for two minutes, and begin to doodle. Again, don't think—just draw.

When time's up, press play on your previous recording. As you listen, make notes, jotting down any keywords, phrases, or answers that strike you. Use these notes to help guide your next move.

CASE STUDIES:

YOU: A wedding photographer

Q: How would you describe your life in one word?

A: Easygoing.

IDEAS: Attract like-minded clients by displaying photos on social media that not only show off my professional work but also highlight my laid-back personality.

YOU: An antique shop owner

Q: If you could live during any decade, which years would you choose?

A: The 1950s and '60s.

IDEAS: Reposition my shop as a destination for mid-century modern goods.

YOU: A lawncare provider

Q: What is your favorite childhood memory?

A: Playing in the tree house that I built with my brothers.

IDEAS: Expand my services by offering backyard tree houses, she-sheds, and he-shacks.

LIST OF QUESTIONS

- **What do you want to do next?**
- What's keeping you from starting the next big thing in your life?
- **Where are you now (physically, mentally, or imaginarily)?**
- How would you describe your life in one word?
- **What is one goal you have for this year?**
- If there were no limitations, what kind of work would you love to do?
- **When there's an awkward pause in the conversation, what do you do?**
- On a scale of 1 to 10, how happy are you?
- **On a scale of 1 to 10, how stressed are you?**
- Would you ever want to live forever? Why or why not?
- **If you could live during any decade, which years would you choose?**
- What adjective best describes how you honestly feel right now?
- **What's the last thing you think about before falling asleep?**
- Do you need structure, or are you a born rule breaker?
- **What can you do today to make your dreams come true?**
- What do you think about when you first wake up in the morning?
- **What qualities make an amazing teacher?**
- Who has always been there for you, no matter what?
- **What's the top excuse that tends to hold you back?**
- What is your favorite way to procrastinate?
- **What tricks help you fall asleep at night?**
- Are you a leader or a follower?
- **Who are your heroes and why?**
- What is your favorite subject to learn about?
- **What gives you creative energy?**
- What do you do to get inspired?
- **How do you sabotage yourself?**
- Where do you see yourself in five years?
- **What is your favorite childhood memory?**
- How do you handle criticism?
- **What scares you?**
- How do you vent your frustrations?
- **What motivates you?**

> **TIP: TWO-FOR-ONE**
>
> Challenge your brain by answering 10 questions as if you were someone else—a friend, a customer, your pet, the president—you get the idea. Notice how your answers change and what stays the same.

ASSIGNMENT:

SAY THAT AGAIN

English

TOOLS: Pen/pencil, paper, thesaurus, pop culture inspiration, a touch of immaturity

EVERYTHING OLD IS new again. Sometimes all it takes is a simple word swap to give a fresh spin to something old fashioned. Case in point: Mad Libs. Before tablets and other boredom-busting media gadgets made traveling with kids much more bearable, less techy generations enjoyed this paper-pad activity on long drives.

When it comes to idea generating, the sort of nonsensical stories and goofy word combos produced by Mad Libs can change the way your brain interprets concepts and objects that have long been familiar. And this new way of thinking can mean a fresh batch of ideas for products, blog posts, apps, headlines, workshop offerings, business services, and the like.

MOTION PICTURE PROMPTS

The following is a selection of movie quotes dating back to the 1950s. As with Mad Libs, fill in the prompts using the parts of speech noted.

1. "_____ your _____, it's going to be a(n) _____ _____."
  [verb]   [plural noun]   [adjective]   [time of day]

2. "Mrs. Robinson, you're trying to _____ _____."
  [verb]   [person you know]

3. "Are you telling me you built a(n) _____ . . . out of a(n) _____?"
  [noun]   [noun]

4. "Have you ever _____ with _____ by the _____ moonlight?"
  [past-tense verb]   [proper noun]   [adjective]

5. "_____ is like a _____ of _____ . You never _____ what you're gonna _____."
  [noun]   [type of container]   [plural noun]   [verb]   [verb]

6. "Yeah, there's like a boatload of _____ at this _____ . This one _____ kept wanting me to join because I'm pretty _____ with a _____."
  [plural noun]   [location]   [noun]   [adjective]   [noun]

7. "If you wear a(n) _____ and have a(n) _____ sidekick, you're a _____."
  [noun]   [adjective]   [noun]

LIGHTS, CAMERA, ACTION

Here's an example of how one prompt plays out on the big screen of ideas. Roll 'em . . .

CASE STUDY: An illustrator wants to design a low-cost item to sell to teachers at his next craft show held at the local high school.

STRATEGY: The illustrator completes the prompts with teachers, school, and students in mind.

FAVORITE PROMPTS:

- "What we've got here is . . . failure to study."
- "Are you telling me you built a whiteboard . . . out of a textbook?"
- "If you wear a mortar board and have a teacher's pet sidekick, you're a principal."

IDEA: A new line of humorous stickers and paper awards teachers and parents can use to help motivate children and positively reinforce good behavior.

SET THE SCENE

Not a fan of our movie quotes? Choose your own! You can also do this with news headlines; book, movie, or song titles; famous quotes; or brand slogans.

WHAT'S MY LINE, ANSWERS:

Curious which movie quotes we used? Here's your silver screen answer key.

1. "Fasten your seatbelts, it's going to be a bumpy night." (*All About Eve*, 1950)
2. "Mrs. Robinson, you're trying to seduce me." (*The Graduate*, 1967)
3. "Are you telling me you built a time machine . . . out of a DeLorean?" (*Back to the Future*, 1985)
4. "Have you ever danced with the devil by the pale moonlight?" (*Batman*, 1989)
5. "Life is like a box of chocolates. You never know what you're gonna get." (*Forrest Gump*, 1994)
6. "Yeah, there's like a boatload of gangs at this school. This one gang kept wanting me to join because I'm pretty good with a bo staff." (*Napoleon Dynamite*, 2004)
7. "If you wear a dress and have an animal sidekick, you're a princess." (*Moana*, 2016)

ASSIGNMENT:

FIELD TRIP

Art

TOOLS: Digital camera,
pen/pencil, and paper

SOME OF OUR favorite school memories are of going on field trips. They allowed us to break free from the humdrum of the too-familiar classroom and explore the world. Ideas don't come from sitting at the same desk looking out the same window every day. It's time to get up and go. We'll lead the way!

HOW TO:

PICK A PLACE. Unless you live in a tiny hamlet, there are probably some places in town you haven't visited. Coffee shops, restaurants, parks, libraries, train stations, and more are waiting for you to take a peek inside. Choose a location where you've never been before. Can't decide? Travel five miles west, and see what catches your eye. (Caution: If a body of water is three miles west of you, go east. Safety first.)

PICK A TIME. For those tiny hamlet dwellers or just diehard creatures of habit, if you disobey rule one and end up at your fave go-to, at least go at a time when you haven't been before. If you typically frequent a tea house in the morning, wait until dark instead. If the place is new to you, choose a time that works best for your schedule.

JUDGE A BOOK BY ITS COVER. Before you embark on your field trip, note what you expect to find at this location. Do you think it will be packed with hipsters? Will the smell of old books linger? How about the scent of freshly baked bread? Will there be a nip in the air or will it be warm and humid?

CLEAR YOUR MIND. With your preconceived notions safely and securely written down, banish them from your brain. Enter the new location with fresh eyes, free of opinions. (That includes any cheeky remarks your inner critic has to say about you. Tell him/her to shut it.)

BE PRESENT. Allow your senses to soak up your surroundings—free of judgment. What do you see? What can you feel? What sounds do you hear? What aromas do you smell? Can you taste anything?

TAKE NOTE. Among your observations, what stands out? Investigate these more closely. Doodle based on your experience. Take pictures to capture the mood or a particular memory you want to dig in to further.

ENJOY IT. Revel in this change of scenery for the new perspective it provides.

HOMEWORK

There was always that one teacher who had to ruin a good field trip by turning it into a teachable moment. Sorry. That's us now. Instead of writing us a 300-word essay on your day out and about, take some time to contemplate how your experience differed from your expectations.

- **How can you apply what you learned and noticed from your field trip to your business?**

- How can your business be applied to the place you visited?

- What trends did you notice that can inspire your work to be more relevant in today's market?

CASE STUDY: The owner of a vineyard has long been offering tours and tastings but wants to offer an on-site experience to encourage more repeat traffic.

FIELD TRIP LOCATION: A craft beer brewery.

FIELD TRIP OBSERVATIONS:

- Beer flights allow for informal tastings, social gatherings, and previews of products. People seem to prefer the more laid-back setting than something more formal.

- Brewery pairs with local animal shelter to raise money and awareness of rescue animals available for adoption. Imbibing is only improved by the presence of puppies and kitties.

- Brewery collaborates with local food carts and trucks to offer food for their establishment without requiring an on-site kitchen and crew.

- Seating is casual and eclectic.

IDEAS:

- Create a wine bar at the vineyard with couches and cozy chairs where patrons can serve themselves using a provided keycard to use with bottles on self-serve taps.

- Ten percent of their beverage purchase can be used toward the purchase of bottles of wine and wine accessories sold in the vineyard or can be donated to a local community organization.

GET IN THE ZONE

Drama

TOOLS: Paper, pen/pencil, colored pencils, clock

WORKING ALONE MEANS productivity is determined by how fast or how slow you go. Some days will make you feel like a real boss, while others will make you think you fell asleep on the job. On the spectrum of work output, most days should fall more in the middle instead of edging on the borders of all or nothing. But when it comes to your moneymaker—the service or product adding to your bottom line—you need to prove your current processes are working for and not against you. To do so, let's diagram your day to see how your actions play out.

A DAY IN THE LIFE OF YOUR WORK

Using the charted example on the following pages, plot out the steps of your work process, filling in every moment from start to finish in 15-minute increments. Be honest and real with your entries; if your grid shows more snack breaks than actual work, own it. This exercise is designed to help you improve your productivity, so embarrassing moments get a pass. Once your grid is complete, analyze your entries using a traffic-light palette of colored pencils and parameters on the following page:

RED LIGHT:

Motivation has come to a screeching halt thanks to distracting activities with virtually no benefit to your workflow.

YELLOW LIGHT:

A slow down happens when tasks requiring minor attention have the potential to sabotage your productivity if your focus isn't dialed in.

GREEN LIGHT:

Productivity is on pace, and you're in the zone where actual paying work gets done.

COLOR CLUES

- Your day should include all three colors, but more green and yellow than red.

- Red is not always bad, just as green is not always good. Sure, all red means no billable hours, but all green and you could be on the verge of burnout. Seek balance.

- Clumping is encouraged. Hold meetings back-to-back to avoid a day of stop and go. Gather your thoughts over a period of time instead of sending lots of one-off e-mails to the same person.

- Learn time-saving tips from your peers at networking events. It's a great way to discover apps and local services that could open up your schedule.

- Discuss your process with vendors and service providers to apply their techniques toward available shortcuts.

- Don't change processes based on one day's data. Repeat this exercise multiple times for a good sampling of time spent.

Time's a ticking! **TURN THE PAGE TO GET STARTED!**

FLOUR POWER PATISSERIE

BEFORE:

	:00	:15	:30	:45
8	Updated inventory spreadsheet.	In need of vanilla, I researched new vanilla vendors.	Found a new party supply site. Everything is so cute!	Created a new recipe based on research I did yesterday for a new flavor.
9	Started prepping dry ingredients in the kitchen.	Took a break to text mom back about her cat's vet visit.	Vanilla vendor's online contact form wouldn't submit—will try again later.	Continued to prep wet ingredients for new recipe.
10	Finished mixing all ingredients together and put the cupcakes in the oven.	Scoped out competitors on social media to see how many events they did this weekend. Shoot! All are doing more than me!	Uploaded cute photo of morning baking session to social media.	Ended up on competitor's website. I need to up my game.
11	Removed the cupcakes and set on racks to cool.	Bride Anna called with changes to her reception desserts.	Whipped up buttercream frosting and topped the cooled cupcakes.	Sent new estimate to Bride Anna including quick inspiration for dessert bar at reception.
12	Hungry! But nothing besides sweets to eat. Heading out to grab takeout.	En route back to bakery.	Ate while scrolling social media posts.	Sent a second e-mail to Bride Anna about another dessert bar idea.
1	Bride Anna called again to discuss e-mails I sent.	Packaged cupcakes and styled a shot for social media. Uploaded immediately.	Feeling inspired. Started looking online for dessert ideas for a baking contest, but ended up researching comfy shoes to wear in the kitchen.	

FLOUR 🌾 POWER PATISSERIE

AFTER:

	:00	:15	:30	:45
8	Updated inventory spreadsheet.	In need of vanilla, I researched new vanilla vendors.	Called my top vanilla vendor pick. The prices were great, so I placed an order.	Created a new recipe based on research I did yesterday for a new flavor.
9	Started prepping dry ingredients in the kitchen.	Prepped wet ingredients.	Mixed all ingredients together and put cupcakes in the oven.	Cleaned up kitchen.
10	Wrote list of things to discuss with Bride Anna.	Called Bride Anna to discuss dessert bar options. Followed up the call with an e-mail including the visual references she requested.		Removed the cupcakes and set on racks to cool.
11	Shot and uploaded cute photo of morning in the bakery to social media.	Scoped out competitors on social media to see how many events they did this weekend. Shoot! All are doing more than me! Oh, well.	Whipped up buttercream frosting and topped the cooled cupcakes.	Packaged cupcakes and styled a shot for social media to use as tomorrow's post.
12	Hungry! But nothing besides sweets to eat. Heading out to grab takeout.	En route back to bakery.	Ate while flagging recipes in new whoopie pie cookbook.	
1	Feeling inspired. Nailed down new menu details to sell next week. Listed all of the flavors of desserts along with the recipes. Listed all ingredients needed using the inventory spreadsheet. Ordered needed supplies.			Made a project time line for the weeks leading up to Bride Anna's wedding.

MAKE THE CUT

Picture your collected grids as if viewing biographical film footage of your life. Play the role of a film director, snipping, moving, and trimming the blocks of your day to improve your flow and increase productivity.

ASSIGNMENT:

HELP YOUR BUSINESS BLOOM

Science

TOOLS: Pencil/pen, paper

BASIC PLANT BIOLOGY might be a distant memory from your middle-school days, but this visualization won't require you to recall the exact purposes of the pistil and stamen. *(Hint: They make the birds-and-bees talk all the more uncomfortable.)* When soil, location, sunlight, and moisture conditions cooperate, a seed has the best chance of growing into a strong, healthy, and beautiful blossom. And as you'll see with this exercise, your small business comes to thrive in much the same way.

CASE STUDY: LET IT GROW

To help illustrate our flower metaphor, we've asked our pretend-friend Violet to let us use her freelance design business as an example. Follow along, labeling your own business in botanical form in order to better identify areas where new ideas could help you grow.

⊙ ROOTS

Roots are the "why" of your business. This is the core reason you are doing what you do.

Violet's Roots:
- my love of art and composition
- a flexible schedule
- making money doing what I love
- working with my dog at my feet

SOIL

Just as a flower won't flourish without nutrient-rich soil, your business needs a nourishing environment.

Violet's Soil:

- a supportive circle of friends and family who encourage, support, and celebrate me
- a group of small-business peers who help to build one another up in the spirit of community-over-competition
- the means to get my work done, including not only my computer, smartphone, office, and design software but also my education, connections, and past work experience

STEM

The stem acts as a support system for the flower, distributing water and nutrients among the roots, leaves, and blooms, while also supplying a strong foundation. Your stem is the "operations" portion of your business—the inner, supportive workings that help keep the lights on.

Violet's Stem:

- creating estimates for clients
- updating my website and social channels with completed projects
- my design process, including knowledge of the software, apps, and digital media
- vendor and contractor relationships
- accounting, budgeting, and invoicing
- administrative tasks to keep my business organized and on track
- calendars and task lists to meet deadlines

LEAVES

Leaves turn sunlight into a yummy food source, which makes them extremely important to the health of a flower. When it comes to your business, your "leaves" are the ways you generate income and other assets.

Violet's Leaves:

- attracting a wider client base by diversifying my offerings beyond just website design to include product packaging, visual identity, marketing print materials, and T-shirt logos

- leading creative workshops for small-business owners to highlight my expertise and network with potential new clients
- extending my income potential by selling complementary products such as digital assets a hobbyist might use when making crafts
- trading my work with other small-business owners, such as an IT professional who helps me maintain my website in exchange for themed website templates

SUNLIGHT

As the flower's actual food, sunlight is essential. In business, your sunlight is the source of your paid work. But just as it's sunny one day, then cloudy for a week, clients and sales come and go. One week, you may have more work than you can handle and another, too little.

Violet's Sun:

- clients
- product sales
- speaking engagements
- workshop ticket sales

WATER

Water helps nutrients travel from the roots to the leaves, which keeps plant cells firm and helps prevent wilting. Just as under- or overwatering affects a plant's health, how you leverage the offerings of your business determines whether it wilts or blooms.

Violet's Water:

- marketing and advertising
- social media presence
- sales calls and meetings
- collaborating with complementing businesses
- volunteering in the community

BLOOM

The bloom—or the pretty part—is the reproductive portion of the plant. Just as a beautiful petals attract pollinators, the "bloom" of your work-world is what attracts customers and clients.

Violet's Bloom:

- my finished work and brand
- attention to detail, deadlines, and customer service
- high praise via client testimonials
- my best work promoted in my portfolio and through other channels
- me!

WEEDS

Weeds aren't technically part of a flower, but they do affect its well-being and longevity. In your business, you probably have plenty of weeds trying to suck you dry or complicate your chances for success.

Violet's Weeds:

- competitors
- budget
- process inefficiencies
- slow-paying customers
- small social media following

UPROOT!

Uprooting your business may seem like a risky move, but it could also be the shake-up your business needs to do its best. In the flower world, transplanting a bloom is a good example of positive disruption. Yes, the uprooting stress could cause the flower to wilt, wither, and die, but its new space could also offer more of the nutrient-rich soil and abundant sunshine it needs to thrive.

Start by listing any and all areas of your business where there's room for improvement. Organize the list in order of priority, keeping in mind which improvements will offer the highest return on your investment (whether you're investing money, time, or physical effort). Now ask the hard, unlikely questions. Your queries will differ according to the situation, but the following are some examples to help you form your own:

- Do I think of my work as "just a job" or as a career?
- What scares me most as a small-business owner?
- What do I wish I'd known when I first opened my business?
- What do I wish I could do more of in my business? Less of?
- What makes me stand out from my competitors?
- How can I improve communication with my clients, vendors, or others essential to the work I do?
- What do I wish potential clients/customers knew about me or my business?
- What do I wish I knew about my audience/clientele?
- If I could relocate to any city, where would my current business be most successful?
- What kind of training or certification would give my business an edge?

With your answers in hand, the last step is to add ideas—the Miracle-Gro, if you will. Use your responses to help you think of creative ways to benefit your business and help it grow healthily and happily.

ASSIGNMENT:

SHOW TUNES

English

TOOLS: Paper, pen/pencil, song, music-playing device, headphones (optional)

IF YOU'VE LISTENED closely to music, then you understand how a tune can affect your mood, bring old memories to mind, and inspire you toward change. Even a wordless melody can communicate information as if it were a language all its own. And if the power of music isn't already apparent to you, this exercise will show you how songs can help solve creative problems.

BALLAD BREAKDOWN

Identify the solution you seek: a new product to sell to teens, an app to cure boredom, a pet salon service. With your objective in mind, think of a song or randomly choose one from a playlist. Listen to that song (or recall it in your mind) and begin listing its aesthetic and emotional elements:

- mood
- theme
- lyric-based imagery
- energy
- colors
- memories

Mix and match the words and scenes you come up with to reach a creative solution. Here's a little ditty we dissected to show you how this can work:

> "IDEAS,
> LIKE LARGE RIVERS,
> NEVER HAVE JUST
> ONE SOURCE."
>
> **—WILLY LEY**

CASE STUDY: Event theme to help collect school supplies and donations for low-income kids

SONG: "You've Got a Friend in Me," by Randy Newman for *Toy Story*

MOOD: Inspiring, loving, supportive, sweet, comforting

THEME: Friendship, solidarity, kindness, dependability, trust, acceptance, support

LYRIC-BASED IMAGERY: Warm bed, old pal, stick together, destiny

ENERGY: Upbeat, happy vibe

COLORS: Pops of primary colors over muted neutrals

MEMORIES: Friendly faces, holding hands, playing on a playground, birthday parties, sleepovers, running through sprinklers, popsicles and ice cream

EVENT THEME IDEAS:

- Buddy Up for Education

- Smile and Say "Cheese" and Wine Night

- PJs and Pancake-Flip Fundraiser

- School Supplies and Sticky Fingers Ice Cream Social

- Candyland Fun(draising) Fair

ASSIGNMENT:

EYE-SPY FLOWCHART

Art

TOOLS: Pen/pencil, paper, camera (optional)

THEY SAY A picture is worth a thousand words—or is it a thousand ideas? Using this classic road-trip game, get ready to open your eyes to a world of ideas hiding in plain sight.

HOW TO:

1. From where you sit, write down one thing that catches your eye, using one or two basic words to define that object. If it helps—and if it won't cause you to look like a creeper—snap a few pics of that item from different angles.

2. Following the diagram style shown, write down three to five words beneath the item that describe it in a little more detail.

3. Keep moving down the flow chart, adding even finer details. If you took a digital photo, zoom in and see what may be harder to detect from far away or with your naked eye.

4. Use the last group of descriptive words as a scavenger hunt of sorts, looking around the room to see what other objects the words you've written down could describe.

5. Think about how those objects could be used to resolve an issue with your small business or creative practice.

CASE STUDY: A cloth-diaper service provider needs to market herself to expecting mothers in order to avoid the struggle of converting those who start out using disposables.

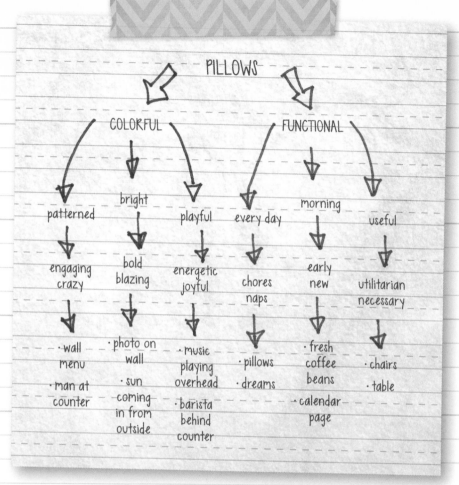

PILLOWS

COLORFUL — FUNCTIONAL

COLORFUL:
patterned → engaging crazy → ·wall menu / ·man at counter

bright → bold blazing → ·photo on wall / ·sun coming in from outside

playful → energetic joyful → ·music playing overhead / ·barista behind counter

FUNCTIONAL:
every day → chores naps → ·pillows / ·dreams

morning → early new → ·fresh coffee beans / ·calendar page

useful → utilitarian necessary → ·chairs / ·table

EYE-SPY OBJECTS: pillows

IDEAS: Expectant mothers are always told how little sleep they will get once their wee one arrives. Play upon this theme, creating an infographic for social media displaying the ways cloth diapers will help moms—and their babies—rest better at night. For example: Sleep easy knowing cloth diapers . . . save you money, which can be put toward your child's future.

- are better for the environment.
- contain fewer harmful chemicals than disposables.
- may reduce diaper rash, keeping your baby's bum happy.
- allow for easier potty training.

AND THE OSCAR GOES TO . . .

Drama

TOOLS: A vivid imagination, someone else's shoes (not literally)

THIS JUST IN: Academy Awards will now be awarded to non-actors for their impressive, everyday accomplishments. And you've been nominated! Congratulations!

OK, your Oscar hopes are still likely next to nil, but imagine what it might be like to accept such a prestigious award for your brilliant performance in *The Movie of Your Life.*

METHOD MAN

Some actors who receive the coveted prize portray characters using method acting. The method actor makes every effort to actually *become* the character he or she portrays by living the experiences of that person—real or fictional—as authentically as possible. That's what we want you to do.

No, you're not playing the role of someone else—just the perfectly imperfect you that you know yourself to be. The only pretend part of this exercise is the golden statue you're in the running to win. So while there's no need to get into character, you do have an acceptance speech to prepare (because there's nothing profound about 30 seconds of stammering improv).

I'D LIKE TO THANK . . .

Imagine hearing your name spoken by Meryl Streep following the magical words " . . . and the Oscar goes to . . . " What milestone in your solopreneur life would deserve such an accolade? Whom would you thank for helping you reach such a momentous achievement? What inspiring words would you share with those who may want to follow on your path?

If dreaming up an acceptance speech for your fake Oscar feels especially silly to you, remember that this exercise serves two purposes: (1) transforming a personal goal into an idea to bolster your business and (2) using visualization techniques to help you make this goal-turned-idea into a reality.

APPLY IT:

Everyone's life movie is different, and each of us aspires to a different sort of Oscar. Here's a list of potential achievements to get you thinking:

- ☆ finally turning a side gig into a main hustle
- ☆ reaching 10,000 followers on social media
- ☆ your business being featured in the *New York Times*
- ☆ hosting a workshop attended by 100 people
- ☆ receiving a celebrity endorsement for your product
- ☆ saying "yes" to following your solopreneur dreams

Don't undervalue what to others may feel small; if it feels big to you, accept your award!

"THE BEST IDEAS START AS CONVERSATIONS."

−JONATHAN IVE

ALL WALKS OF LIFE

Science

TOOLS: Comfy shoes, camera, computer, pen/pencil, paper, fresh eyes

EVEN IF YOU'VE lived in your neighborhood for decades, there's always something new to see if you just look hard enough. From small improvements to a neighbor's once-dated home to the impact seasonal weather has on the grass in your local park, constant flux is part of life.

To avoid letting life pass you by, take a walk and open your eyes to the tiny changes—and great big ideas—that are all around you. Explore your neighborhood—or other destination—by capturing it in photos using these pic tips:

DON'T OVERLOOK THE FAMILIAR. Street signs, fire hydrants, fences, and mailboxes may all seem old hat, but they're just like snowflakes: no two are alike.

CHANGE YOUR PERSPECTIVE. Zooming in or out on your camera can dramatically alter the way a common item appears. When taking a picture of a tree, for example, zoom in tight on the bark. Instead of photographing a flower from above the bloom, give an ant's perspective from underneath the petals.

HUNT FOR HUES. Feeling overwhelmed . . . give yourself a mission. For instance, limit yourself to the color blue. Soon you'll have shots of the sky, robins' eggs, mailboxes, yard decor, siding, and so much more.

COMPARE AND CONTRAST. Think all stop signs look the same? Take a series of pictures of signs on different streets to see just how unique each red octagon can be.

TRACK DOWN TEXTURE. Surfaces lend interesting depth and create cool shadows when the light is right. Instead of focusing on an object's shape or color, try capturing its texture.

PICTURE PATH

It's go-time! Set a time or distance goal for your walk, and take as many pictures as you can within those parameters. Now, off with you. We'll meet you back on the next page when you've finished pounding the pavement.

WELCOME BACK, WANDERER!

If you're anything like us, then your walk has helped to clear your mind, scrap some stress, and stimulate your soul. Feels good, doesn't it?

With a renewed pep in your brainstorming step, let's put those pictures to work. Upload your images to your computer and view them on the screen. Select nine photos from the bunch (either randomly or by playing favorites). Place them in a three-by-three grid, as shown above. *(Note: You can do this in most word processing documents or using a web template in which to upload your images.)*

GALLERY GOER

Now, let's pretend you're an art critic attending a gallery opening featuring the work of a budding photographer. Throw on a black turtleneck, pour yourself a glass of red wine, and begin to analyze your images by answering these questions:

- What similarities do you detect among these images?

- How would you describe this display in one word or phrase?

- What qualities draw you to these images, and what qualities repel you?

- What questions come to mind when you see this set of images?

- Which two images feel the most similar? Why? Which two feel the most different from one another?

- Who among your friends or family members would these picture most impress? Why?

Now ask questions that get to the heart of your objective:

- If these images were an advertisement for a book, what would the book's title be?

- If you had to create a commercial using these images, what product would you be selling?

- If these images were framed and hanging as a collection in someone's home, how would you describe his or her style?

- Which cocktail would pair best with these photos?

- Using the clothes in your wardrobe, which outfit would best complement these images?

- If you had to plan an event using these images as inspiration, what party theme would you select?

- If these pictures represented a vacation destination, where would it be?

CASE STUDIES: Allow the prompts to guide you toward ideas. Here are a few ways this could play out:

- An event planner uses the photographic inspiration to develop a unique, upscale menu for a corporate event.

- A calligrapher designs a new style of script to use for the signs she makes and sells in her online shop.

- A home stager discovers a soothing color palette to use when decorating clients' homes for sale.

- A personal trainer designs an outdoor beginners' workout to offer as a free promotion for people in the neighborhood.

WEATHER ADVISORY

As natives of Wisconsin (a.k.a. the frozen tundra), we totally get that taking a walk isn't always in the cards. When Mother Nature puts a hard stop on your outdoor plans, rely on your existing photo library. And maybe just march in place while perusing in order to get that creativity-boosting blood flow going.

ASSIGNMENT:

STRING THEORY

English

TOOLS: Paper, pen/pencil; optional: wooden beads, cording, scissors, fine-point marker

ACTUAL STRING THEORY is light-years beyond our pay grade. Thankfully, this activity has nothing to do with particles and everything to do with stringing together words to create themes from which names, products, services, activities, applications, process improvements, and more can follow. If you're feeling especially crafty, grab some lettered beads and string your word combos along some pretty-colored cord. Bonus by-product: super-nerdy jewelry.

STEP 1: *Choose This or That.*

Choose one item from each of the this-or-that pairings.

THIS		THAT
cake	or	doughnut
comedy	or	thriller
city	or	country
coffee	or	tea
food truck	or	diner
bound book	or	e-book
formal	or	casual
painting	or	photo
drive	or	fly
hands-on	or	digital

STEP 2: Make a Chain.

Choose three words from among your selections and string them together randomly—like beads on a bracelet. For example: cake + country + painting.

STEP 3: Get Creative.

With the words strung together before you, listen for idea clues.

Idea: A summer camp for kids offering art classes in rural settings. One project could include cake decorating using items from nature.

STEP 4: Repeat.

Keep the ideation session rolling along by linking new sets of words using others you selected or by creating all-new selections. Try adding a fourth, fifth, or even sixth word to a set to see how that changes the ideas it inspires.

APPLY IT: STRUNG OUT

Whatever the words may be, make them work for your idea objective. Here are a few examples:

- A freelance writer pitches a local city guide an article on "The Nine Best Places to Snap a Pic on Chicago's Michigan Avenue" based on the sequence "city + photo + drive."

- From the words "cake + painting + digital," a baking supplies business owner creates a new line of printable icing templates inspired by the floral headbands of Frida Kahlo.

- The owner of a boutique public relations agency turns the chain "tea + bound book + digital" into "Tea and Tomes," an online Q&A session authors can use to engage with their readers when promoting their books.

ASSIGNMENT:

COLOR SWATCHING

Art

TOOLS: Scissors, glue stick, paper, various papers for cutting (magazines, paint chips, catalogs, old maps, junk mail)

COLOR IS POWERFUL. It can evoke moods, influence buying decisions, tempt appetites, and stimulate learning. Often, certain colors are associated with particular things or feelings. For example, red often connotes heat, anger, passion, or blood, while blue is frequently associated with sadness, refreshment, a sense of calm, or even truth.

An entire language exists within the giant box of crayons you may have cherished as a child. A color on its own may have plenty to say, but combine it with another, and you get a story.

COLOR THEORY 101

If it's been a while since you took a spin around the color wheel, let's do a quick review.

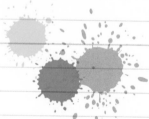

Analogous: very similar, cohesive colors

Complementary: colors opposite one another on the color wheel, which helps to make each pop

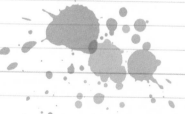

Pastel: soft, muted tones

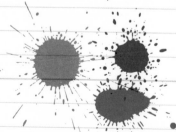

Bold: bright, energetic tones

APPLY IT: THE COLOR OF IDEAS

You may think color is important only for painters, website designers, interior decorators, or makeup artists, but the truth is a good color story can inspire so much more: a presentation topic, a menu special, a teaching method, or a seasonal bouquet.

HUES FOR YOU

Ready to give it a try?

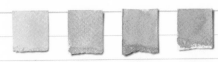

- Define your idea objective.

- Cut out swatches of single colors from the various papers noted in the supply list.

- Lay the colors out on a flat surface, and begin to pair colors randomly.

- Pick your favorite pair and build on it by adding one or more additional swatches.

- When you've landed on a palette, ask yourself the following questions:

  - What emotions does the group of colors convey?

  - What things (people, cultures, places, objects, foods, experiences) do these colors remind you of?

  - How can these colors help you reach your idea objective?

PALETTE BINDER

Don't have a specific objective in mind but want to have some fun combining colors? Turn this activity into an icebreaker and save your color pairings in a binder to call upon when you need inspiration in an instant. You could also takes pics of your palettes and store them digitally. Next time you're in need of color inspiration for a social media post or vibe for your next podcast episode, flip through to find the colors that move you most.

WISHFUL THINKING

Drama

TOOLS: Pen/pencil and paper

REMEMBER WHEN YOU were a kid and you wished you had a robot that would clean your room or a computer program that would write your book reports for you? Now that you're all grown up and the adulting struggle is real, we bet you've got a whole new list of inventions you'd like to see on shelves: refrigerators that magically stay stocked with favorite foods, dryers that deliver the laundry already folded, and furniture surfaces that dissolve dust on contact.

As outlandish as these ideas may seem, remember that there was once a time (and not so long ago) when telecommunication seemed like a hairbrained fantasy. Turns out, if you can dream it up, someone, somewhere, sometime can probably make it real.

CASE STUDY: DREAM IT

Write your creative challenge or idea dilemma in the center of a piece of paper. Now, let your imagination run free and write each of your fantastical inventions on a cloud. Remember, the crazier your ideas are, the better!

A train that could safely travel across oceans

Human teleportation devices

OBJECTIVE: A self-run travel agency wants to provide trip ideas for people who hate flying on airplanes but still want to see the world.

Flying cars

A teleportation pill you take before bed so that you fall asleep in your bed but wake up at your travel destination

Dorothy's ruby slippers: just click your heels together and be dashed away to your destination

A travel agent genie to grant your vacation wishes

DO IT

All right, daydreamer, it's time to get your head out of the clouds and make it rain. And by that, we mean choose one of your "inventions" and think of realistic ways to achieve its aim. Write each of your ideas on a raindrop.

A travel agent genie to grant
your vacation wishes

A travel website offering
completely preplanned trips
where no flying is required

A calming travel pillow
infused with lavender and
chamomile essential oils

An app that alerts you of
travel deals for destinations
available by car, rail, and boat

A virtual-reality experience
that allows you to explore the
sounds, smells, and sights of new
destinations from your own home

A business that combines
travel planning and wellness to
offer trips designed for people
who like to go places but are
uncomfortable getting there

Repeat the rainy-day exercise with each of your clouds for a full-on flood of doable ideas.

TODDLER TIME

Science

TOOLS:

Childlike wonder

REMEMBER BACK TO when you were a kid and the great big world around you—even just your own backyard—led to nothing but endless wonder. "Why is the sky blue?" you might've asked, or, "Why do dogs bark and birds chirp?"

As an adult, if you've spent any time with children, you know that their list of questions goes on and on and on and on . . . and then on some more. However amazingly insightful your responses, all your answers seem to do is prompt more probing.

Take a cue from the kiddos in your life by borrowing this technique. Come up with a question relating to your idea objective. Rather than answer the question, follow it with another related question. Answer that question with a question, and so on. Your goal is to challenge assumptions and dig deeper into the unknown until your inner child's curiosity is satisfied. Here's how this might look:

CASE STUDY: A web developer wants to increase her competitive edge without lowering her prices.

[Q] What are your current customers' web needs?
[A] A website.

[Q] What kind of website?
[A] One that meets the needs of their businesses and clientele/customers.

[Q] What do you currently offer?
[A] Coding, hosting, programming language, technology knowledge, project management, product development, creative problem solving, and so on.

[Q] Which of your current offerings do you most enjoy?
[A] Creative problem solving.

[Q] Why?
[A] It allows my brain to work in a different way than other parts of my job require.

[Q] How so?

[A] A lot of web development I do can be very formulaic, and the step-by-step process can feel repetitive.

[Q] Is repetitive bad?

[A] Not bad. Just not always challenging.

[Q] Is challenging good?

[A] The right kind of challenging is.

[Q] What's an example of the right kind of challenging?

[A] When a client wants to add functionality to the site that is outside the norm.

[Q] What does that mean for you?

[A] It can mean learning new skills or researching how to tweak existing functionality to make it work in a different ways.

[Q] How does this benefit you?

[A] My breadth of knowledge expands, meaning I have more to offer my client and other clients in the future.

[Q] How does this benefit your client?

[A] My client gets a website that works exactly the way he or she wants without having to contract another expert, which saves money. It creates an almost one-stop shop.

[Q] Why is a one-stop shop good?

[A] For the customer, it means having to work with only one person instead of playing go-between among different vendors. For me, it means increasing the amount of money I can charge, because I'm adding more value.

[Q] What other website components could be added to a one-stop shop?

[A] Content, design, graphics, images, marketing automation, and so on.

[Q] Are these services you could offer?

[A] I have a lot of knowledge of web design, and maybe with a few extra classes I'd feel comfortable offering this service.

[Q] Learning presents a challenge, right?

[A] Yes.

[Q] Is it a good kind of challenge?

[A] Yes.

[Q] So how about signing up for those classes so that you can increase your service package?

[A] Good idea!

ASSIGNMENT:

THAT'S THE WORST!

Art

TOOLS: Paper, pen/pencil, coloring supplies (colored pencils, markers, or crayons), a warped sense of reality

FEEL LIKE YOU'RE coming up with only bad ideas? Awesome! Let's make them even worse! As unproductive and silly as this approach may seem, thinking of the "worst possible solution" to a creative problem can help you uncover the good solution that's often just beneath the surface.

BAD, WORSE, WORST

As usual, start by defining your idea objective. Remember that for the sake of this exercise, your solution needs to be pretty inadvisable. Unsure how to go bad? Consider the following approaches:

- offend someone (remember, you're not sharing this)
- do things the lazy way
- ignore customer service
- encourage sarcasm and snide remarks
- lose money—even give it all away
- cause harm (again, this is just pretend!)

REALLY BAD ADS

Now up the intensity of this exercise by mocking up an ad that mocks good ideas. Write out a commercial script or marketing slogan. Perhaps illustrate a poster with your terrible idea.

HAIRY JOHN'S BARBER-SHOP

WHEN YOUR BEARD NEEDS GROOMING, LET US MAKE IT YOUR FAVORITE—AND ONLY—FEATURE.

CASE STUDY: Barbershop wants to attract men with facial hair.

WORST IDEA: Make facial hair the only feature of the face.

LEARNING MOMENT

Now that you've gotten THAT out of your system, be prepared for good ideas to rise up in protest!

THE TAROT OF IDEAS

English

TOOLS: Pen, paper, deck of cards, beginner's luck

WE'RE NO TAROT experts, but this activity won't require any training in the occult arts. When it comes to ideas, even a standard deck of cards can help you divine your idea future.

HERE'S HOW TO PLAY:

- Define your idea objective.
- Divide the deck of cards by suit and shuffle each pile.
- Slip the Joker cards into two of the piles and reshuffle them.
- Select the top card from each pile and lay it face up in front of you.
- Decipher your cards using the categories shown below.

DIAMONDS = *Person*

A: waitress
2: librarian
3: 5-year-old boy
4: mother of young children
5: dog owner
6: college-aged athlete
7: comedian
8: teenage girl
9: hipster
10: barista
J: grandfather
Q: pilot
K: ballet dancer

CLUBS = *Place*

A: mountaintop
2: beachside hut
3: busy city street storefront
4: small-town cafe
5: tent
6: warehouse
7: movie theater
8: tree house
9: subway station
10: truck stop
J: dock (pier)
Q: storage shed
K: school

SPADES = *Things*

A: shirt
2: clock
3: book
4: coffee
5: tire
6: plant
7: grass
8: rattle
9: carpet
10: water
J: jewelry
Q: ukulele
K: rice

HEARTS = *Proper Nouns*

A: Alps
2: Chicago
3: Declaration of Independence
4: Disney World
5: Starbucks
6: London
7: Airstream
8: New York Yankees
9: Oreos
10: Martha Stewart
J: Labor Day
Q: Jupiter
K: Southwest Airlines

JOKERS: *Wild!* Select any word you like.

DRAW YOUR DESTINY

With your idea objective in mind, use the four words pulled from the deck to come up with a "reading" that inspires or solves your creative solution. You don't have to use the exact words pulled from the cards in your reading (though you certainly can!). Instead, think about how the words and concepts presented might come together to suggest a theme or thought pattern. Take the following hand as an example:

Using the nouns, "**BARISTA, TENT, WATER,** and **LABOR DAY,**" here's how a couple of readings might sound according to the idea objective in play.

CASE STUDY: Craft beer brewery needs an idea for a new recipe to put on tap.
READING: A new camping-inspired brew is in your future: Golden Sky Glamper, a blonde coffee ale brewed with purified water.

CASE STUDY: Massage therapist wants to offer a seasonal service to encourage past clients to rebook.
READING: A summer of camping on rough terrain has fed your soul but strained your back. Beginning this Labor Day weekend, sooth and energize your aching bones with a Coffee Bean Body Massage, featuring a scrub handcrafted for your skin type.

KNOW WHEN TO FOLD 'EM

If the deck isn't in your favor, don't be afraid to fold your hand and pull new cards. (After all, this isn't a real tarot reading.)

THE IDEA AT THE END OF THE TUNNEL

Drama

TOOLS: Paper, pen/pencil

AS WE MENTIONED on page 37, it's important to think of constraints—or obstacles—as opportunities. That goes for the obstacles you face personally as well as those you observe others facing. For this exercise, let's consider the constraints produced by the oh-so-common habit of frivolous spending.

Begin by listing common ways people overspend or spend frivolously. Here are a few to get you started:

- unused gym membership
- eating out too often
- buying brewed coffee
- shopping online

BREAK IT DOWN

It's safe to assume, barring a few A-listers with mountains of money to misuse, most people would prefer not to fritter their cash away. Cha-ching! Herein lies a creative opportunity. To start, select one of the common habits above, and list its advantages and disadvantages. Then look for opportunities for improvement.

Here's how this might look if you choose "shopping online."

ADVANTAGES: What are the benefits of shopping online?

- ease and convenience
- broad selection and variety
- allows you to easily compare products
- no lines or crowds
- can ship gifts directly to the recipient

DISADVANTAGES: Flip the script. What are the disadvantages of shopping online as it pertains to spending?

- shipping costs
- impulse purchases
- costly returns
- increased risk for fraud

- returns are a hassle, so undesirable or defective products are never sent back
- hidden fees

OPPORTUNITIES: How might you mitigate the disadvantages or compete with the advantages?

- Set online limits to avoid spending over a certain amount.
- Be warned when hidden costs, fees, or automatic subscriptions are involved.
- Improve the in-store convenience and variety.

- Create a return method that doesn't involve shipping.
- Offer more "try before you buy" options.
- Build a "thinking time" feature into carts whose contents might qualify as impulse purchases.

BUILD IT UP

Great! You've identified the opportunities. Now it's time to create the solution. Begin by listing possible applications. Then move on to high-level ideas.

APPLICATIONS: What options, technological or otherwise, do you have for delivering these opportunities?

- app
- software
- phone call
- text

- e-mail
- snail mail
- physical product
- human

IDEAS: Pair opportunities with applications to develop a list of high-level ideas.

- A "Sleep-on-It" browser extension that allows you to fill your cart but forces you to wait 48 hours until you can check out.

- A budget app that acts like a special checking account dedicated to online spending. You can set caps according to item type (for example, clothing, books, housewares, electronics, food), which would block unnecessary purchases.

- A handheld scanner that allows you to shop in the store without having to stand in line.

Don't stop now! **WHAT OTHER EVERYDAY PROBLEMS CAN YOU DISSECT?**

BRAIN BREAK: *Stick with It*

It's hard to imagine what brainstorming was like before Post-it Notes came on the scene. But it wasn't until 1974 that these slightly sticky squares came to be—by complete accident.[2]

A NOT-SO STICKY SITUATION: In 1968, scientist Dr. Spencer Silver was tasked with producing an adhesive with super-stick power. Instead, he ended up with a substance at the opposite end of the tacky spectrum. Yes, it was sticky, but it never formed a lock-tight bond. While this more removable adhesive wasn't what Silver was after, he knew it might serve a different purpose, so he shared his creation with a few trusted friends.

HYMNAL HEADACHE: Meanwhile, Silver's scientist peer, Art Fry, had a daunting personal dilemma of his own. During his weekly church choir practices, Fry would mark the hymns to be sung at the next service using scraps of paper as bookmarks. But by the time Sunday arrived, the markers would shake loose, causing Fry to lose his place and have to flip furiously through the pages.

THE AHA MOMENT: Fry remembered Silver's accidental adhesive discovery and came up with the idea for sticky but removable bookmarks. Eureka!

PARTNERING ON PERSPECTIVE: Together, Fry and Silver developed what we now know as Post-it Notes. Their story remains a perfect example of how "mistakes" can be fruitful. It's also a great case for sitting on an idea until the proper application presents itself.

"THE AIR OF IDEAS
IS THE ONLY AIR
WORTH BREATHING."

—EDITH WHARTON

5 SIT & SIMMER

WITH YOUR BEVY OF BRIGHT IDEAS BREWING, TAKE A BREAK TO ALLOW THE BEST ONES TO RISE TO THE SURFACE.

LET IT BE

AFTER ALL THAT brainstorming, you're probably itching to put your best idea into action. As inspired as you may feel, it's important to take a break and let your idea simmer for a while. Don't run with it, don't start ordering supplies, and definitely don't share your breakthrough on social media. Set your idea aside and return to your regularly scheduled life.

Think of it like gardening. It's no accident that putting an idea into someone's head (or your own head, for that matter) is often referred to as "planting the seed." A lot goes into planting a seed: finding the ideal container, selecting a location with optimal sunlight, prepping the soil, digging a resting spot at the perfect depth, and so on. But once you've done the necessary prep, the rest is up to chance—or fate, depending on how you see things. No amount of poking or prodding or wishing or agonizing will make your seed sprout any faster. While you'll need to water the surrounding soil, do it too much or too often and nothing will grow.

An idea is no different. Sure, you can give it some thought and maybe even research online to see if someone has already discovered and had success with a similar concept. But it's important to give your idea a chance to take root. Harvest it too quickly and you're likely to waste effort, time, and money.

We're aware that this "sit and simmer" time may trigger some (totally normal) anxiety. To stem the stir-craziness, we've filled a whole chapter with activities to help you calm your mind, get clear about your intentions, and prepare you for the work that's to come.

ROCK YOUR GOALS

The sit and simmer stage is a great time to set some new goals for yourself. If mention of "goals" causes you to clam up, remembering your latest failed New Year's resolution, you're not alone. In fact, only about 8 percent of us actually achieve what we set out to do on the first of the year. Why is that? Let's take a moment to consider some common reasons people don't reach their goals:

- Lack of time
- Too many distractions
- Loss of interest
- Lack of control
- Lack of resources or knowledge
- Self-sabotage
- Lack of motivation
- Too much stress
- Lack of a plan

Or, in a word: *Life.*

Face it: goals are hard. They're often too rigid and therefore extremely vulnerable. A single bump in the road can easily derail even your best-laid plans. So, what if we told you there was an easier and more effective approach to achieving your aims? No joke, friends—there is. We like to call it the "Why—not What—Method."

LOOKING FOR THE "WHY"

Most New Year's resolutions are some version of the following:

- Eat healthier
- Exercise more
- Spend less

What's wrong with these goals? They focus on the "what," as in what you'll do, rather than the "why," the reason you want to do these things.

So, ask yourself:

Why do I want to spend less?

So I can have more money.

Why?

So I can fix the house.

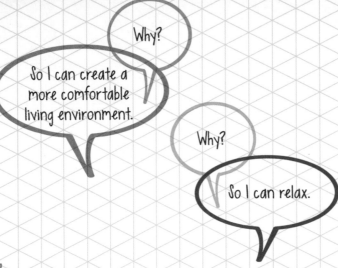

Boom. Perhaps your real goal is to relax. Spending less may help you get there, but there are lots of ways to relax that have nothing to do with how much or how little you spend.

THE PROBLEM WITH A PLAN

Most goal experts emphasize the importance of making a plan—because setting a goal without making a plan is like embarking on a road trip without a map or GPS. That is, if you think of your goal as a destination.

If your goal is to spend less, your plan might include these action steps:

- Pack a lunch
- Clip coupons
- Eat out less
- Cut cable
- Shop secondhand
- Carpool

Each of those action steps requires its own set of sub-steps. For example, if you choose to clip coupons, your subplan might be to map out your meals for the week based on the coupons you've collected, which then requires you to look for recipes that include the discounted items, which then requires you to make a grocery list, which then requires you to take an inventory of your pantry, which—you get the point.

In short, your plan quickly becomes complicated. It's definitely doable, but it will require a lot of time, motivation, resources, and all those other things whose absence tends to prevent us from achieving our goals.

So, again, look for the "why." Instead of trying to spend less, focus on relaxing more. When your goal is about the "why," all of the busywork of planning disappears, and so do the most threatening obstacles to your success.

◉ ROCK IT

Once you've drilled down into your own goals, choose a word or short phrase that sums up your "why." Now get crafty and paint your word or phrase on a small rock—one that can sit at

the corner of your desk, or hang out in your pocket, as a reminder of what motivates you. If your rock says "RELAX," you might glance at it during moments of high stress and consider what you can do—or stop doing—in that moment, to chill the heck out.

Have more than one "why"? Consider painting several rocks and collecting them in a basket. Blindly draw one out each morning and let it serve as your intention for the day.

RE-ZEN YOUR ZONE

We need to talk about your desk again. Kudos if you took our advice on page 18 and turned your work space into a textural wonderland rivaling the She-bicle. But just as your desk space can help or hinder creativity, it can also ignite or inhibit your killer work instinct.

#1 Get Clean: When it comes to concentration, it's best to tidy up the casual chaos. Toss those crumpled-up papers peppering your desk into the trash for two points a shot.

#2 Lighten Up: Low light may be best for brainstorming, but brighter is better when your goal is to slay tasks.

#3 Seat Yourself: Turn the tables on your brain by changing where you sit in your office. If you always sit facing east, see what westside story your desk has to tell.

#4 Stash Some Stuff: If you've got lots of doo-dads littering your desk, consider scaling back as the brainstorm dials down. Tactile distractions are great for idea-generating, but less so when it's time to put those ideas into action.

#5 *Bring Back the Bean:* While too much java can inhibit creativity, a bit of caffeine may be the thing that helps refocus your wandering mind.

#6 *Invite Ideas:* Just because you've cleared your desk, turned up the lights, and had a cup of coffee doesn't mean ideas won't still come knocking. Without ignoring them completely, let them hang out in a waiting room of sorts. Keep a notebook open on your desk for jotting down those rogue creative thoughts—and revisit them when you're not tending to more pressing matters.

THERE'S A POSE FOR THAT

Want to increase your willpower? There's a yoga pose for that. Boost your confidence? There's a pose for that, too. Reduce self-consciousness? Get inspired? Fire up your creativity? Influence positive change in the world? You guessed it—there's a pose (and more than likely, multiple poses) for all these things and more.

In an effort to help you clear your mind and prepare to dig deeper into your ideas, we've selected poses that are specifically designed to inspire focus.

PRAYER POSE

Stand tall with your feet about hip distance apart. Bring your palms together and your thumbs to your sternum. Close your eyes and set your intention. For the purposes of this section, make focus, concentration, or mental clarity your goal. Breathe in and out of your nose deeply yet gently for 10 to 12 breath cycles.

HERO POSE

Kneel on the floor with your knees together. Create a space between your feet that allows your booty to sink toward the ground. If this is too hard on your knees, place a pillow or rolled up blanket under your bum to help prop you up. Keep your spine nice and tall and rest your palms on top of your thighs. Close your eyes or gaze softly down the tip of your nose, breathing for five breath cycles.

TREE POSE

Let's play with balance. If you tend to be a wee bit wobbly, try this pose next to a wall or stable chair for support. With your feet, shift your weight onto your right foot, and lift the heel of your left foot off the ground. Slowly bring your left sole to rest at your inside right ankle with your toes on the floor, on your inner right calf, or your inner right thigh (but never to your inner knee). Hands can be on your hips, at prayer position in front of your sternum, or lifted straight overhead. Hold this position for three to five breath cycles before repeating it with the opposite leg.

Disclaimer: We are not yoga instructors. If any of the following poses cause you pain or discomfort, you should stop immediately.

MIND-BENDING MOVES

If you've never done yoga before, you may assume it requires ballerina-like flexibility. While it's true some yoga poses seem to call for rubber joints, the ones in this section are appropriate for everyone, including total beginners.

Don't worry about creating a "flow" from one pose to the next. Simply start a new posture when you are finished with the previous one. If you have a yoga mat, great; roll it out. But a carpeted floor will also do. If you're slipping and sliding too much, consider wearing socks with sole-grips. Otherwise, just wear comfy clothing that allows for movement.

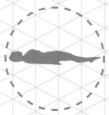

KNEE-TO-HEAD POSE

Sitting on the floor with your legs in front of you, bring your left sole to the inside of your right thigh. Bending forward from the hips (but not rounding the upper back), tilt forward to try to touch your head to your knee. If you're not quite there yet, don't force it. Just tilt forward until you can feel a gentle stretch. Close your eyes and hold for five breath cycles before repeating the pose with the opposite leg.

CAMEL POSE

Begin kneeling with your knees about two fists' width apart and your upper body tall. Place your palms on the top of your booty with fingers pointing toward the ground. Keeping your head and neck relaxed, bend backward as if your shoulders and upper back were curving around a beach ball. In this position, make sure to tuck your tailbone under as you push the front of your hips forward. You can stay here, or take things up a notch by lowering your hands to grip your heels. Stay in this position for three breath cycles before slowly returning to an upright position.

CORPSE POSE

Lie flat on the floor with your palms facing up at your sides. Let all your muscles relax. Close your eyes and take a moment to concentrate on your breath. As random thoughts enter your mind, notice them and let them pass. Stay in this position for a minute or two—or longer if you're up to the challenge. (Psst: It's not as easy as you think!)

JAZZERCISE YOUR BRAIN

Just as it's important to stretch before physical activity, it's important to warm up your brain before putting it to work. Try these simple brain games to train your noggin for sharpness and agility.

MIRROR MOUSE

Sometime when you're not chasing a deadline, try using your mouse with your nondominant hand. Doing so activates the opposite side of your brain, which can improve how well information is communicated between your mind and hand.[1]

HEAD STANDS

You know those framed photos of loved ones on your desk or office walls? Flip 'em upside down. This simple trick will cause your brain to send out an alert that helps improve how quickly you pick up on little details in your environment.[2]

CHAT AMONG YOURSELF

Having trouble remembering your elevator pitch or what you want to present at your next workshop? Try talking to yourself. Science shows that saying the words out loud versus saying them silently in your head can improve your memory of them.[3]

HUE CAN DO IT

In preschool, you probably played games involving sorting objects by color. While sorting activities are especially educational for toddlers, they can also help adults make sense of the world around them. Take a look around your office, and begin sorting items by color. Fill a mason jar with all blue writing utensils and another with all red, or organize your bookcase by spine color. These fun and simple activities can help you organize both your work space and your thoughts.

GET PERSONAL

Working alone may allow you to call the shots, take all the credit, work uninterrupted, and enjoy your very own private bathroom. However, depriving yourself of social interaction (the kind that doesn't involve scrolling) can actually dull your cognitive capabilities.[4] Build moments into your day that offer quick exchanges with other human beings. Consider chatting with a neighbor when fetching the mail, ordering your tea from a barista instead of brewing your own mug to chug, or asking for advice from your library's research desk instead of relying solely on the Internet.

BLIND MAN'S BLUFF

Try going about one of your everyday activities (preferably one that doesn't involve a hot stove or heavy machinery) with your eyes closed. You may be surprised to find that even conducting a client phone call blind can help to sharpen your other four senses—and challenge your brain to think in new ways.[5]

DRAWER TEASER

Open a desk drawer and scan the items for up to one minute. Close the drawer and try to write down as many items as you can remember on a sheet of paper before checking to see how you did. If the game is too easy, add more items to the drawer. If it was too hard, keep practicing . . . or maybe consider purging old office supplies.[6]

IS IT TIME YET?

Only you will know when it's time to fully commit to your idea. Like any good, supportive friend, we hope you won't go rushing into something that will ultimately break your heart. We just want you to be happy! So, we've created a little game to help you decide whether you're ready to take the plunge.

THE CHECK-IN CHECKLIST

Check off the items below and add up your score at the bottom.

Since my last lone brainstorming session, I . . .

- ☑ ate a meal. (1 point)
- ☐ took a shower. (1 point)
- ☐ had a good night's sleep. (1 point)
- ☐ watched a movie. (1 point)
- ☐ read a book. (1 point)
- ☐ took a walk. (1 point)
- ☐ made a craft. (1 point)
- ☐ updated my to-do list. (1 point)
- ☑ talked to a friend. (1 point)
- ☐ practiced mindfulness. (5 points)
- ☐ tried yoga poses for focus. (5 points)
- ☐ cleaned my desk. (5 points)
- ☐ set a new "why" goal for myself. (5 points)
- ☑ painted my goal on a rock. (5 points)
- ☐ exercised my brain. (5 points)
- ☐ completed a deadline project. (10 points)
- ☐ volunteered my time to a community or nonprofit organization. (10 points)
- ☐ took a vacation. (10 points)

TOTAL SCORE: _ _ _ _ _ _ _ _ _ _

Turn the page for your next move.

YOUR MOVE

1 TO 10 POINTS: THINK AGAIN

Where do you think you're going? Heed our sage (and safe) advice and put in a bit more time before you invest yourself in your idea.

11 TO 24 POINTS: NOT SO FAST

Hold your horses, partner. You're making progress, but before you saddle up, why not put in a little more "me" time?

25 TO 38 POINTS: PROCEED WITH CAUTION

Go ahead and dip your toe in the pool of your idea. If that feels OK, begin wading into the shallow end. Remember: NO DIVING ALLOWED!

39 TO 51 POINTS: SAFE ZONE

Nice! You've made quick work of the sit and simmer! Continue along your path.

52 TO 69 POINTS: FULL SPEED AHEAD

Congratulations! Your patience level is seriously impressive. We are confident that this is the beginning of a beautiful relationship between you and your big idea. May you enjoy a lifetime of innovative bliss together!

HANG IN THERE!

You're almost done!

6 DEBRIEF

CHANNEL YOUR INNER PSYCHOLOGIST
AND ANALYZE THOSE IDEAS TO
BEST SELECT "THE ONE."

DECISIONS, DECISIONS

WOOHOO! THE SIT and simmer is officially over, and you are ready for work mode. There's only one thing left to do: confirm which idea you're ready to make happen.

While you were probably brimming with ideas immediately following the brainstorm stage, it's likely that the sit and simmer led to some natural culling. Perhaps . . .

- Someone beat you to the idea punch.

- You realized that your idea would require more work than you're able to put in.

- You currently lack the money or resources needed to make your idea a reality.

- You simply lost interest.

- The organized chaos that is your office finally caught up with you, and your documented ideas have disappeared.

- While you were sitting and simmering, you realized that your idea wasn't as great as you initially thought. (The brainstorm is over—judge away!)

The main goal of the sit and simmer is to lighten your idea load so that choosing a project doesn't feel like picking fifth-grade dodgeball teams: Do you select the strongest player who's sure to dominate but operates like a drill sergeant? Or do you pick your not-so-athletic bestie who probably won't help you win but makes the game a blast to play?

If you're lucky, your choice will be obvious and you can set to work straightaway. But for most of us, brainstorming exercises don't result in a clear winner. Which is why it's important to cap your choices.

ROUND ONE: The Gut Cut

Getting input from trusted family and friends about your ideas is important, but as a solopreneur, your most essential debriefing companion is your own gut. Your stomach has a lot to say if you just take the time to listen. We've all had butterflies in our stomach, experienced a gut-wrenching blow, or had our stomach tied up in knots. Decoding your tummy's signals can go a long way toward understanding how you *really* feel about an idea.

Use the spectrum below to help sort your ideas according to how each affects your abdomen. If you find an idea gives you a "troubled tummy," go ahead and strike it from your list.

GUT CHECK

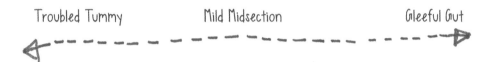

Troubled Tummy   Mild Midsection   Gleeful Gut

ROUND TWO: Follow the Stars

Back before maps—let alone GPS—explorers often looked to the skies for guidance. It turns out a bit of stargazing can also help you navigate even the densest sea of ideas.

Start by writing each idea from the "Mild Midsection" to "Gleeful Gut" zone on its own individual sticky note.

Place the sticky notes together in a place where you can view them all at once (for example, a wall, a large table, the floor, a window).

Label each idea based on the following criteria:

 STAR: Ideas that feel most practical and achievable. Move these ideas onto Round Three.

 MOON: Ideas that might require more resources, time, or energy than you have at the ready—but that you're still over the moon about. These ideas might not be as strong as the stars, but put them through to Round Three to see if they can prove their worth.

 COSMOS: Pie-in-the-sky ideas that might not be possible right now but are worth circling back to another time. Set these ideas aside for another time. You've got stronger ideas to focus on in the meantime.

OBJECTIVE: Custom wood sign vendor wants to increase annual sales and profits.

Create themed gifts featuring a wooden sign and related product to sell at local boutique shops.

Host in-home wood-sign painting parties.

Renovate a camper and use it as pop-up sign shop to sell locally and while traveling.

Sell original wooden signs at regional craft shows.

ROUND THREE: *Get Picky*

Now that you've narrowed the field, it's time to choose your top three finalists. Here's how:

TWO OR THREE STARS: If the previous step left you with just two or three starred ideas, congratulations! Your work here is complete. Move ahead to the final round.

TOO MANY STARS AND MOONS: If you're still left with more than three ideas from which to choose, it's time to get picky. Using the chart that follows, analyze each remaining idea in terms of the effort it requires and its potential for success.

Winner's Circle: High Success, Low Effort	High Success, High Effort
Sell original wooden signs at regional craft shows.	Host in-home wood-sign painting parties.
Low Success, Low Effort	Low Success, High Effort
Create themed gifts featuring a wooden sign and related product to sell at local boutique shops.	

The best finalists will likely come from with the Winner's Circle, but your goals and motivation could dictate otherwise. If you still have more than three ideas at this stage, run your narrowed-down ideas through Rounds One through Three as many times as needed until you have your set finalists.

FINAL ROUND: *Date Your Ideas*

After swiping left on a number of ideas, it's finally time to swipe right. But with two or three potential idea mates from which to choose, let's gather more information before you settle on "the one."

Imagine how each of your ideas might respond to the following dating questionnaire. Feel free to customize the questions or add new queries to get to the heart of your objective.

· I'm really good at:

· Five things I can't go without:

· In one year, I see myself:

· In five years, I see myself:

· I meet the needs of others by:

· When it comes to money, I can manage on:

· Must-have technology for me:

· When it comes to working one-on-one or on a team, I prefer:

· A commercial about my strengths would feature:

· I have a weakness for:

· I dream of changing the world by:

· The social media platform that best captures what I have to offer is:

· From profit, awareness, goodwill, solution, and efficiency, the word that best describes my best possible outcome is:

· What sets me apart from other ideas is:

· When it comes to fun or commitment, I prefer:

DECISION TIME

You've tested your gut, consulted the stars, charted the potential, and gone on a first date. It's time to commit!

If you're still on the fence, take a moment to read and meditate on the following quotations and do a bit of journaling in response.

> "COURAGE IS RESISTANCE TO FEAR, MASTERY OF FEAR, NOT ABSENCE OF FEAR."
>
> —MARK TWAIN

· Fear is a completely natural response to challenge. Is fear causing you to feel stuck? If so, what scares you about your ideas, and how might you "resist" or "master" those fears?

> "WHEN YOUR DREAM IS BIGGER THAN YOU ARE, YOU ONLY HAVE TWO CHOICES: GIVE UP OR GET HELP."
>
> —JOHN C. MAXWELL

· Would your idea become more doable if you asked for help from others? Whom could you ask?

> "CREATIVITY TAKES COURAGE."
>
> —HENRI MATISSE

· Perhaps you're not quite ready to commit, and that's OK. Take some more time to sit and simmer.

If you've found the one, then...

Congratulations
On Your Big Idea!

NOW, CELEBRATE! POP OPEN A BOTTLE OF BUBBLY, TREAT YOURSELF TO A NIGHT ON THE TOWN, OR SETTLE IN FOR A LUXURIOUS TWO-HOUR NAP. DO WHAT FEELS RIGHT!

THEN, ONCE YOU'VE PROPERLY MARKED THIS AMAZING MILESTONE, MOVE AHEAD FOR A BIT OF IDEA INSTRUCTION.

YOUR IDEA: THE OWNER'S MANUAL

MAINTENANCE

Just as your car requires routine maintenance, so does your idea. Follow these instructions to help keep her running smoothly.

- Get to know your idea like no one else can. The more you know about it, the better you can respond to its needs, wants, and challenges.
- Accept your idea for the weirdo it is. Other people may laugh at your idea or say it's a waste of time. Ignore the cynics and move ahead despite their unsolicited criticism.
- Protect your idea. Protection may mean keeping your idea to yourself and waiting for the perfect time to reveal it to the world. Or it may mean taking legal and financial measures to guarantee that no one can steal, duplicate, or harm your idea.
- Properly nourish your idea. Feed your idea the attention, time, and effort it needs to thrive.
- Give your idea room to grow. Prepare for your idea to morph over time, and be patient as it grows and changes.

TROUBLESHOOTING

A new idea is a lot like a new romantic relationship. In the beginning, it's all rainbows and butterflies, but after a while, you might find yourself feeling frustrated, stressed, exhausted, or bored.

When the going gets tough, try these quick fixes:

WALK AWAY. Take a break—short or long—before abandoning your idea completely.

FORGET FEARS. If you're in a rut, consider whether a particular fear is keeping you down.

REVISIT OBJECTIVES. It's easy to get mired in the nitty-gritty and lose sight of the bigger picture. Pull out that painted rock from page 105 or simply remind yourself of your "why" goal.

ADAPT. As your idea shifts and changes, so must your method for bringing it to life. Don't be afraid to reroute as needed.

WHEN GOOD IDEAS GO BAD

Let's face it—sometimes it just doesn't work out. Not every relationship is worth saving, and not every idea is worth hanging on to. That said—many are. Use this flowchart to help you decide whether it's really time to call it quits.

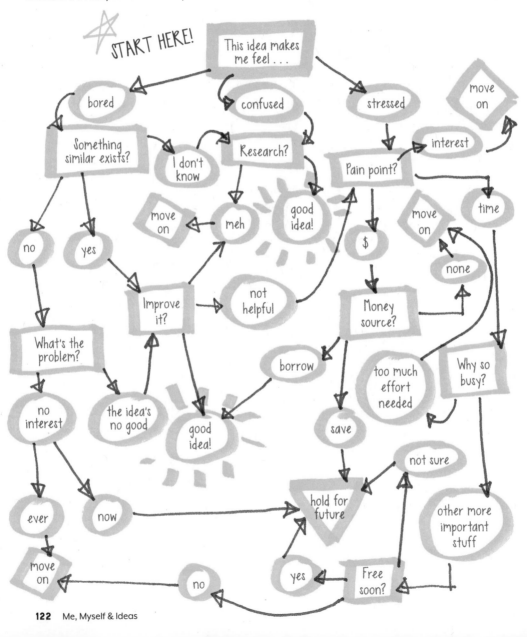

GOOD IDEA

There's still plenty of life in your idea, so don't give up on it just yet. Consider why it's not sitting well with you at the moment and address those issues, which may include:

- your availability
- knowledge, training, or skills needed
- accessible resources, funding, or extra help
- something similar already exists in the marketplace

SAVE FOR LATER

Just because you lack time, resources, or interest doesn't mean you should ditch an idea entirely. You may just need a bit more time to sit and simmer. Or you may need to tuck this one away until you're ready to give it the attention it deserves. Keep old ideas on file (in an actual file cabinet, in a file on your computer, or simply scrawled in your journal). Make a point to check back in after a certain period of time (days, weeks, months, years) and give your old ideas a second chance.

MOVE ON

Some idea partnerships just aren't meant to last. The sooner you can cut your losses, the more quickly you can dedicate yourself to a new idea. But before you toss your old idea out with the garbage, consider recycling it. Try sending your idea to a friend for whom it might make a better fit, or break the idea down into "good" and "bad" parts and see what can be salvaged.

"THE UNIVERSE
BURIES STRANGE
JEWELS DEEP
WITHIN US ALL,
AND THEN STANDS
BACK TO SEE IF WE
CAN FIND THEM."[1]

—ELIZABETH GILBERT

KEEP THE IDEAS COMING

The act of brainstorming, by yourself or in a group, is a very intentional way of sparking new ideas. If we've done our jobs, then at any point, you can follow the steps laid out in this book to generate solutions to any creative problem.

While seeking ideas intentionally serves its purpose and has its place, let's not ignore the perks of the spontaneous idea sessions mentioned earlier in the book, like those times when showers, chores, commuting, and standing in long lines cause ideas to fall from the sky without any exerted effort. This passive process sounds like a lazy (wo)man's game of which you have no control, and that's true to the extent you can't rely on spontaneity to deliver ideas on demand. But there are ways to help encourage curiosity, creativity, imagination, and ingenuity in your daily life so that surprise ideas drop in more often.

> "IT ALWAYS SEEMS
> IMPOSSIBLE UNTIL
> IT'S DONE."
>
> —NELSON MANDELA

PUZZLE SOLUTIONS FROM PAGE 50:

LIVE A CREATIVE LIFE

When you want to live a healthy life, you make better food choices, you move more often, you cut back on the adult beverages, and if you have more willpower than the Wonder Women, you eliminate sugar. At first these actions will feel foreign, and you'll naturally want to resist and go back to what you know best—eating pizza and drinking wine while lounging on the couch. However, the more practice you put in toward replacing bad habits with good, the easier you find it is to live that healthy life.

Replace "healthy" with "creative," and while the steps you take will differ, the scenario is quite similar. The more creativity you welcome into your world, the better your ideas—intentional or spontaneous—will be. It, too, will feel foreign to add creativity to a day usually spent fully in front of a screen with the same mass of tabs competing for your attention. However, with time, practice, and a little patience, your tendency to resist will fade and the actions will soon become part of your regular routine.

Not sure how to make your day more creative? There are plenty of ways, whether you have two minutes or two hours.

- Complete one icebreaker each day regardless of your brainstorming intentions.
- Create a visual-thinking journal.
- Snap a photo at the same time every day.
- Read a children's book.
- Draw something using a doodle-a-day prompt.
- Make a Play-Doh sculpture.
- Color a picture.
- Bake (and eat!) cookies.
- Solve a crossword puzzle.
- Jump rope.
- Sit quietly outside and just listen.
- Make an animal from a balloon.
- Play an instrument.
- Blow bubbles in your backyard.
- Listen to a new podcast.
- Sing a song.
- Create hand-drawn mandalas using a Spirograph.
- Write a poem.
- Draw your morning in comic-strip form.
- Create a new knock-knock joke.
- Read a paragraph backward.
- Design a vision board.
- Swing on the swings at the park.

GOOD LUCK!

WELL, FRIEND, WE'VE REACHED THE END OF OUR
JOURNEY TOGETHER. IT'S TIME FOR US MAMA BIRDS
TO NUDGE YOU OUT OF THE NEST AND INTO THE GREAT
BEYOND—WHERE WE'RE CONFIDENT YOU'LL KEEP AFLOAT,
BUOYED BY THE POWER OF YOUR OWN IDEAS.

ACKNOWLEDGMENTS

FROM *the Wonder Women*

Despite being two ladies who like to be in control and always be right (both of which we never really are), we were immensely happy to let a few people take the reins. To our agent Alison Fargis and her Stonesong crew, thank you for sticking with us and using your incredible talent and tenacity to find the perfect home for our beloved idea. We are in awe of the passion and humor you infuse into your work. Despite the lack of age difference, we want to grow up to be you someday!

Thank you to Andrews McMeel Publishing for giving two solopreneurs the opportunity to inspire big ideas in others. In doing so, you've allowed more awesome people into our lives, specifically, Melissa Rhodes and Holly Stayton. Melissa, you're an amazing editor, and this book is all the better thanks to your sharp eye, expertise, and dedicated efforts. Thank you for all you do. Holly, we love that you're among our tribe of idea people. Brainstorming with you is more fun than work, and we love seeing our book through your lens of optimism. You inspire us!

Last, running our small business may be on us, but we'd be in much rougher shape without our cheerleaders who encourage, motivate, and help us. Thank you to the Madison business community for welcoming and supporting us. You guys rock! And a special thank you to those who've played a direct and important role in Wonder and this book: Sarah Jane Boecher for helping us crush our proposal; Gina Beebe for the inspirational mentor you always prove to be; Anne Adametz for helping to keep our crazy in check (we know it's no easy feat, friend!); Stacey Anderson for being our biggest fan; and Emily Balsley for being our creative partner in crime. We couldn't do it without you all!

FROM *Carrie*

Tattooing the name of the one you love on your body is said to jinx a relationship, but I hope the same isn't so for giving someone top billing in the book acknowledgments. Because, honestly, Shane, I can't imagine my life without you. There's no one else with whom I'd rather lounge around and watch sports, *Seinfeld* reruns, and documentaries. You're my favorite person with whom to buddy up to the bar when day drinking on weekends (and some weekdays, too). Thank you for catching me when I fall, which my klutzy self (physically and mentally) does quite a bit. I love our perfectly imperfect life together.

To Dexter, the world's most awesome bulldog: you can't read this, but mama loves you, your snuggles, your clowny ways, and even your stink. You'll always be my good boy.

I'm blessed to have a life filled with amazing friends. To list you all and how you each make me whole would take its own book. Please accept a simple thank you and typed hug for what should be so much more! That said, I must call out the Inner Circle. Barbara, Jodi, Kaia, and Meagan, I'm forever grateful for the foundation of laughter, support, love, solidarity, and ridiculousness on which we've built our crazy clubhouse. I can't imagine a world without you amazing women!

To the mother of all mothers-in-law, thank you, Rose, for making me your Baby Girl. You not only created the man who holds my heart but also fill my world with unconditional love. Our shared laughter, tears, and talks are the makings of treasured memories.

All families have their special breed of crazy, and mine is no exception. Whether you're a sibling, in-law, or extended relative, you've shaped my world. Thank you to my parents for fueling the drive and resolve that have led me to be the creative, independent woman I am today. You were my first lesson in the necessity of big dreams and hard work. I wouldn't love my life today without you. And a special shout-out to Sean. You once cheered me on to poop on the potty with readings of

The Berenstain Bears, and today you still swell with pride over my accomplishments, big and small. You're a great big brother. Writing a book is no joke. Stress almost took me out of the game a few times, but this ol' gal made it through with a little help from her new besties: Tylenol, Prilosec, and Ben and Jerry's Karamel Sutra. (And no, I receive no commission from these endorsements . . . though, they are certainly welcome!)

Last, this book wouldn't be possible if it weren't for Jessica, my creative-, chocolate-, and all-things-'90s-hip-hop-loving bestie. Thank you for being the up to my down, the joy to my WTF?, and the friend I never knew I couldn't live without. I hope we never forget what we love about one another . . . but with our failing memories, I wouldn't bank on it! Our friendship is our best idea yet.

FROM Jessica

It's been said that parents should provide their children with roots and wings. My parents have given me both of those in spades. To Mom and Dad, I am grateful for your everlasting love and support no matter what crazy ideas I spring upon you!

To Dan and Liam, you two are my reason for hustling! Thanks for providing love and laughter when I need it most. You're my heart!

To my sister, Shannon, I'd probably be drowning under a pile of papers and dust (and tears) if it weren't for all of your help in keeping me sane. I love you!

To all of those who continually inspire me, especially Ivy Ross. Ivy, thank you for the innovative approach to idea generation within big companies. I am forever grateful for my time with you at Mattel. Not only are you a creative motivator but your kindness and joy radiate. Thank you.

Finally, to Carrie, there's no one with whom I'd rather journey through this work life. You're the yin to my yang, the bread to my butter, the milk to my cookies. You . . . *wait for it* . . . complete me.

ENDNOTES

SECTION One

1. "'Boaty McBoatface' Polar Ship Named after Attenborough," BBC News, last modified May 6, 2016, http://www.bbc.com/news/uk-36225652.

2. Sara Mednick, Ken Nakayama, and Robert Stickgold, "Sleep-Dependent Learning: A Nap Is as Good as a Night," *Nature Neuroscience* 6, no. 7 (June 22, 2003): 697–8, https://doi.org/10.1038/nn1078.

3. Alex F. Osborn, *Your Creative Power: How to Use Imagination* (New York: Charles Scribner's Sons, 1949), 269.

SECTION Two

1. Global Workplace Analytics, "2005–2015 American Community Survey," Global Workplace Analytics, http://globalworkplaceanalytics.com/telecommuting-statistics.

2. Jeffrey Rossman, "The Mood-Boosting Effects of Light," in *The Mind-Body Mood Solution: The Breakthrough Drug-Free Program for Lasting Relief from Depression* (New York: Rodale, 2011), 92–4.

3. Anna Steidle and Lioba Werth, "Freedom from Constraints: Darkness and Dim Illumination Promote Creativity," *Journal of Environmental Psychology* 35 (September 2013): 67–80, https://doi.org/10.1016/j.jenvp.2013.05.003.

4. Ryan Rahinel, Joseph Redden, and Kathleen Vohs, "Physical Order Produces Healthy Choices, Generosity, and Conventionality, Whereas Disorder Produces Creativity," *Psychological Science* 24, no. 9 (August 1, 2013): 1860–7, https://doi.org/10.1177/0956797613480186.

5. Roger Ulrich, "The Impact of Flowers and Plants on Workplace Productivity Study," Texas A&M University in College Station, Texas, "About Flowers," last modified March 4, 2011, https://aboutflowers.com/quick-links/health-benefits-research/workplace-productivity-study/.

6. Ravi Mehta, Rui (Juliet) Zhu, and Amar Cheema, "Is Noise Always Bad? Exploring the Effects of Ambient Noise on Creative Cognition," *Journal of Consumer Research* 39, no. 4 (December 1, 2012): 784–99, https://doi.org/10.1086/665048.

7. Michael J. Glade, "Caffeine—Not Just a Stimulant," *Nutrition* 26, no. 10 (October 26, 2010): 932–8, https://doi.org/10.1016/j.nut.2010.08.004.

8. Glenn Enoch, *The Nielsen Total Audience Report: Q1 2016* (New York City: Nielsen Company, 2016).

9. Matthew A. Christensen, Laura Bettencourt, Leanne Kaye, Sai T. Moturu, Kaylin T. Nguyen, Jeffrey E. Olgin, Mark J. Pletcher, and Gregory M. Marcus, "Direct Measurements of Smartphone Screen-Time: Relationships with Demographics and Sleep," *PLoS One* 11, no. 11 (November 9, 2016): 6–9, https://doi.org/10.1371/journal.pone.0165331.

10. Ullrich Wagner, Steffen Gais, Hilde Haider, Rolf Verleger, and Jan Born, "Sleep Inspires Insight," *Nature* 427, no. 6972 (January 22, 2004): 352–5, https://doi.org/10.1038/nature02223.

11. Lorenza S. Colzato, Ayca Szapora, Justine N. Pannekoek, and Bernhard Hommel, "The Impact of Physical Exercise on Convergent and Divergent Thinking," *Frontiers in Human Neuroscience* 7 (December 2, 2013), https://doi.org/10.3389/fnhum.2013.00824.

12. Trine Plambech and Cecil C. Konijnendijk van den Bosch, "The Impact of Nature on Creativity—A Study among Danish Creative Professionals," *Urban Forestry & Urban Greening* 14, no. 2 (2015): 255–63, https://doi.org/10.1016/j.ufug.2015.02.006.

13. Carol Clark, "A Novel Look at How Stories May Change the Brain," ScienceDaily, last modified January 3, 2014, https://www.sciencedaily.com/releases/2014/01/140103204428.htm.

14. Stephanie Lichtenfeld, Andrew J. Elliot, Markus A. Maier, and Reinhard Pekrun, "Fertile Green: Green Facilitates Creative Performance," *Personality and Social Psychology Bulletin* 38, no. 6 (March 16, 2012): 784–97, https://doi.org/10.1177/0146167212436611.

SECTION *Three*

1. Janina Marguc, Jens Förster, and Gerben A. Van Kleef, "Stepping Back to See the Big Picture: When Obstacles Elicit Global Processing," *Journal of Personality and Social Psychology* 101, no. 5 (2011): 883–901, https://doi.org/10.1037/a0025013.

2. Ravi Mehta and Meng Zhu, "Creating When You Have Less: The Impact of Resource Scarcity on Product Use Creativity," *Journal of Consumer Research* 42, no. 5 (October 1, 2015): 767–82, https://doi.org/10.1093/jcr/ucv051.

SECTION Four

1. "How Many Words Are There in English?" *Merriam-Webster* online, accessed May 23, 2018, https://www.merriam-webster.com/help/faq-how-many-english-words.

2. "History Timeline: Post-it Notes," Post-it Brand, accessed on September 17, 2018, https://www.post-it.com/3M/en_US/post-it/contact-us/about-us/.

SECTION Five

1. Lawrence C. Katz and Manning Rubin, "14 Weird Brain Exercises That Help You Get Smarter," *Reader's Digest*, accessed May 17, 2018, https://www.rd.com/health/wellness/brain-exercise/.

2. Arti Patel, "Brain Exercises: How to Stimulate Your Brain and Senses," HuffPost Canada, last modified December 13, 2012, https://www.huffingtonpost.ca/2012/10/15/brain-exercises_n_1966861.html.

3. Noah D. Forrin and Colin M. MacLeod, "This Time It's Personal: The Memory Benefit of Hearing Oneself," *Memory* 26, no. 4 (October 2, 2017): 574–9, https://doi.org/10.1080/09658211.2017.1383434.

4. Lawrence C. Katz and Manning Rubin, "14 Weird Brain Exercises That Help You Get Smarter," *Reader's Digest*, accessed May 17, 2018, https://www.rd.com/health/wellness/brain-exercise/.

5. Lawrence C. Katz and Manning Rubin, "How Neurobics Work," in *Keep Your Brain Alive: 83 Neurobic Exercises to Help Prevent Memory Loss and Increase Mental Fitness* (New York: Workman, 2014), 49–55.

6. Devika Garg, "Concentrating to Jog Your Memory," NeuWrite West, last modified June 4, 2015, http://www.neuwritewest.org/blog/2015/6/4/concentrating-to-jog-your-memory.

SECTION Six

1. Elizabeth Gilbert, *Big Magic: Creative Living Beyond Fear* (New York: Riverhead Books, 2015), 8.

Me, Myself & Ideas

Andrews McMeel Publishing
a division of Andrews McMeel Universal
1130 Walnut Street, Kansas City, Missouri 64106

www.andrewsmcmeel.com

19 20 21 22 23 TEN 10 9 8 7 6 5 4 3 2 1

ISBN: 978-1-4494-9628-9

Library of Congress Control Number: 2018947961

Editor: Melissa Rhodes Zahorsky
Art Director: Diane Marsh
Production Editor: Amy Strassner
Production Manager: Tamara Haus
Photo credits: pages iii, v, 1, 13, 16–17, 18–19, 20, 22–23, 24–25, 31, 40, 51, 52–53, 63, 80, 85, 89–90, 95, 97, 101, 106–107, 108–109, 110, 113, 120, 126, 134 © Getty Images; pages x and 127, Melissa Vaughan Photography; page 105, photos and styling by Emily Balsley; page 128 (top right), Natural Intuition Photography; page 129 (bottom), Ruthie Hauge Photography

ATTENTION: SCHOOLS AND BUSINESSES
Andrews McMeel books are available at quantity discounts with bulk purchase for educational, business, or sales promotional use. For information, please e-mail the Andrews McMeel Publishing Special Sales Department: specialsales@amuniversal.com.